FIERCE GENIUS

Andy Bollen

FIERCE GENIUS

Cruyff's Year
at Feyenoord

First published by Pitch Publishing, 2021

Pitch Publishing
A2 Yeoman Gate
Yeoman Way
Worthing
Sussex
BN13 3QZ
www.pitchpublishing.co.uk
info@pitchpublishing.co.uk

A CIP catalogue record is available for this book
from the British Library.

ISBN 978 1 78531 824 5

Typesetting and origination by Pitch Publishing
Printed and bound in India by Replika Press Pvt. Ltd.

Contents

This book is dedicated to
Johan Cruyff.

Fierce Genius is a cinematic look
at the career of Johan Cruyff, seen
through the prism of his final season
as a player, spent at Ajax's bitter rivals,
Feyenoord.

Andy Bollen

Introduction

HENDRIK JOHANNES Cruijff – Johan Cruyff to you and I – in full flow, was often compared to a great artist, a Dutch Master, a maestro or maverick. Why wouldn't he be? He was Dutch. He shared the same rain, sunshine and light as Vincent van Gogh, Rembrandt and Vermeer.

When the Dutch football legend Johan Cruyff (the native spelling confused too many outside of the Netherlands) is discussed and pored over by sports journalists, his style of play is regularly elevated to an art form. We shouldn't be surprised. When writers contemplate Cruyff's play in detail, there is a natural inclination to compare his athleticism to the form, movement and creativity of the greatest works of art.

If art truly is an interplay between the artist, the world and the means of figuration, then Cruyff's brand of football, one of exquisite technique, fluidity and movement, confirmed it: Cruyff *was* an artist. He had the temperament of an artist and performer. A pervading obsessiveness for excellence, like Buddy Rich, Picasso or Leonard Bernstein, fixated with greatness, self-improvement and an at times impossibly high level of expectation.

His personal life was packed with as many inciting incidents as his playing and coaching career; moments almost as intriguing as his stunning level of performance and his many twists and turns. The fluidity of his story often seems as complex as Cruyff's football intelligence; a constantly moving, chess-playing strategist, when he would create a move deep in his half, and end it, 20 passes later, knowing where the play would end, scoring in the opponent's six-yard box. However, real-life events would become as interesting as his football and come to shape the story of his life.

Here was an iconic figure, an imperious sportsman, the epitome of style, invention, creativity and 1970s glamour. He wasn't only playing football; he was re-imagining it. Yet away from the game, when he wasn't in control, the scene shifted, his dramatic intensity had no release, and chaos ensued.

In October 1977, aged 30, Cruyff quit international football. While in his Barcelona apartment, Cruyff, his wife Danny Coster, and three children were subject to a kidnap attempt. The experience changed his attitude to life and became part of the reason he decided not to play in the 1978 World Cup. He revealed the story in an in-depth interview, in 2008, for Catalunya Radio: 'You should know that I had problems at the end of my career as a player here. I don't know if you know that someone put a rifle at my head, tied me up and tied up my wife in front of the children at our flat in Barcelona.'

Cruyff managed to escape but the incident affected him. 'The children were going to school accompanied by the police. The police slept in our house for three or four months. I was going to matches with a bodyguard,' he continued, his normally confident voice becoming troubled. 'These things change your point of view ... there are moments in life in which there are other values. We wanted to stop this and be a little more sensible. It was the moment to leave football and I couldn't play in the World Cup after this.' Cruyff was done, he'd had enough of kidnap threats and yet there was worse to come.

Sick of the game, the pressure of superstardom and relentless travel, when his contract ran out at the Nou Camp, he had made up his mind. He was retiring, from the game completely, aged 31. By March 1979, his Barcelona flat was repossessed. This stemmed from two financial issues. Firstly, he was almost bankrupted after being scammed into poor investments in property and a pig farm (Cruyff had made the biggest financial mistake of his life and was robbed of his fortune).

Secondly, there was a major tax issue with Barcelona. The club's incoming president, Josep Lluís Núñez, and Cruyff did not get on. In the future, Núñez would bring back Cruyff as head coach, purely for political gain and it helped guarantee he would remain president but that's for another chapter. For now, all we need to know is the tax rules were changed for players and the clubs had a long-standing agreement where they helped players meet the shortfall. Since Cruyff had already announced his retirement at the end of the season, and wouldn't be a Barca player the following year, Núñez refused to pay Cruyff's substantial shortfall and the player was left to pay the sizeable bill himself.

Cruyff's agent, manager and father-in-law, Cor Coster, was one of the first super-agents who negotiated deals and transfers; he also represented Johan Neeskens when he moved from Ajax to Barcelona. While playing, Cruyff hardly saw his agent-manager-father-in-law, spending most of his time playing, training or travelling. But once retired he had nothing to do with plenty of time on his hands and money in the bank. The pig breeding scam would cost dearly and change both the impetus and dynamic of his story.

In business, if you are in any doubt, most would stay away, but Cruyff, as the press loved to suggest at the time, was too pig-headed. If in doubt, leave it out. If you do invest at least have some kind of interest or passion for it; invest in wine, art, or in Cruyff's case, something connected to sport.

When Cor Coster checked his client's finances and wanted to know what he had done, Cruyff tried to remain nonchalant, hoping to deflect the inevitable. He told Coster he had bought three plots of land to build on. When Coster immediately demanded to see the deeds of the land he had bought, Cruyff couldn't provide any. The reality dawned on him. He wasn't used to dealing in business transactions. He was a football player; he had been done. Coster's advice was blunt, first as an agent, and then a father-in-law: 'You've been shafted. You've paid for it but there is nothing in your name. Get the whole business out of your head. Accept your losses and then go and do what you're good at.'

The loss was substantial. Having signed for Barca in 1973, for a then world-record transfer fee of $2m (£929,000), the wages and tax arrangements were far more amenable than his package as an Ajax player. Of the wage difference itself, Cruyff would say, 'The salary on offer was gigantic. At Ajax, I was earning a million guilders a year.' Furthermore, in the Netherlands,

Cruyff paid close to 72 per cent in taxes. At Barcelona, it was different. 'I was earning twice as much and only paying 30–35 per cent to the Spanish tax man. I wasn't just earning more. I was getting to keep more of it.'

Between a considerable wage increase, a decrease in his taxes, not to mention endorsements and sponsorship deals, between 1973 and 1978 Cruyff would have amassed a considerable amount. Coster did not trust the conman, Michel Georges Basilevich, suspecting from the moment he came on the scene that he was a thief, and he was proven right. But his daughter and son-in-law were besotted with the reputedly charming Russian-Frenchman. They thought they had acquired property, stately buildings, businesses and invested heavily, and ultimately badly. Basilevich was given complete control of Cruyff's fortune and proceeded to burn through the footballer's money. It was blown in months. Businesses they had invested in folded immediately. The pig farm investment in Ganadera Catalana was the business which grabbed the headlines. In his autobiography, *My Turn*, Cruyff explains, 'I believe that everyone has a destiny, a fate, of his or her own. Mine was probably to leave the game at a young age, do something phenomenally stupid, then find my feet as a footballer again. In fact, that's the whole story of my playing career in three lines.'

Despite countless requests to reconsider and play for the Dutch side in Argentina, he declined. He refused to leave his family at home in 1978 for the World Cup. Cruyff explained he was okay with the decision until invited by the BBC to add his considerable insight as a pundit for the organisation's coverage of the final between the Netherlands and the hosts. Maybe his competitive juices were flowing? Throughout the action, he felt sick, and suffered greatly while watching the game, thinking he should've been with his team-mates. Watching it analytically and having to comment as a viewer hit him hard. He realised he might have been able to help the side win. He would later say, 'Would we have won if I had been there? I think, quite honestly, that we might have done. Because my qualities, even at that point, would still have added value to the team.' Cruyff later explained, 'We were a bit further on as a team than in 1974. I could have joined in but I chose not to. Then at the BBC, I found myself thinking, damn, I would really have liked to be there. It was all very strange and rather sad.'

If anything, when you listen to him at this time, it sounds like he was already starting to regret quitting and being out of the game. In conversation, he sounds lost and off-kilter. It would also be idiotic to assume Cruyff would ever have been able to affect the game and win the World Cup in Argentina. He would not have known this as he watched from the safety of the BBC studios. The outcome had been decided before the competition started, by the murderous military junta who ruled the country.

The trouble didn't lie with the Argentina players; it wasn't their fault. Argentine manager César Luis Menotti (as Cruyff played his final season for Feyenoord, Menotti was coach at Barcelona) later explained, as momentum grew in the competition, he had to cajole his more principled players into forgetting about generals and play for their families, and the real people of the country, the bus drivers, bakers and miners.

In 1986, the *Sunday Times* alleged that in 1978, Peru were bribed before their game with Argentina, which the hosts needed to win by four clear goals to reach the final. They did. Then there was also the ferociously intimidating nature of the crowd on the way to the stadium for the final. The Dutch team bus, for some reason, was deliberately taken on a lengthy and tortuous route through Buenos Aires to the stadium, where it was subject to a barrage of violent attacks by Argentine fans.

Once they reached the Estadio Monumental, the Dutch were made to wait for the kick-off, while Argentina became showbiz divas, playing further mind games, keeping not only their opponents waiting but the world too, looking on in disbelief at the lack of organisation. It felt like it was taking the hosts an age to appear. It was only five minutes, but with every second, the partisan crowd of 71,483, mostly Argentine fans, were allowed to raise the temperature further, and hurl more abuse at the Dutch.

Once the players did appear, the crowd were frenzied, then Argentina complained and famously demanded a cast worn by the Netherlands' René van de Kerkhof was removed, this despite the player having worn it on his wrist and played throughout early games. The referee forced him to have it bandaged up and cover it. By this point, the Dutch threatened to walk off the pitch. Even Johan Cruyff might have struggled, though we will never know.

Cruyff consistently repeated he simply didn't know exactly how much was lost in total through the financial scam. He refused to focus in any great detail about the losses over this period, only saying he lost most of his property and a lot of money. He always shrugged it off and was vague about the figure. He was a proud, competitive man and it was his business. The press consistently referred to a figure of $6m, which would conservatively equate to $24m today. Once you understand how Cruyff's mind works, that would most likely be a low estimate. It is far likely a higher figure and the situation more perilous than what he would reveal.

Yet there was something in his mentality that allowed him to shrug it off, to turn the disadvantage into an advantage and move on from the tax issues and horrendous business moves. The most important lesson taken from the whole debacle became clear: his business was football.

When he came out of retirement, a chain of events was set in motion which would bring us to this book, and his year in Rotterdam, playing for Feyenoord.

Cruyff's retirement from the game would not last long. Within seven months, he was back playing in the United States, first with LA Aztecs then the Washington Diplomats. After a move to English side Leicester City fell through, he played briefly for Levante, in Spain. He returned to Ajax, signing in December 1981, won the title, then the following season won the league and cup double. In 1983, aged 36, after Ajax failed to renew his contract, he moved from there and headed to arch-rivals Feyenoord.

When the player passed away in March 2016, he may have found it comforting to know he lived to see Josep Lluís Núñez being investigated and eventually jailed for corruption for attempting to bribe tax officials inspecting his construction business. One of Cruyff's lasting legacies was his insistence

Barcelona renovate and place more focus on their La Masia youth academy which would create and develop a golden generation for the club. Núñez's legacy, despite everything he would bring to FC Barcelona, was somewhat tarnished by his dramatic final scene; being jailed for corruption.

Chapter 1

Even in his Youth ... Love of Ajax

THE VERY notion of someone born, bred and growing up in the shadow of a club and dreaming of playing for his team seems so alien now. Football, and with it, wider society has changed. Yet few words get real fans more excited than hearing 'one of our own' is coming through the youth setup. The very concept of a player showing so much promise being guided through the ranks, coming through every age group, who not only lived around the corner from the club but was steeped in the very fabric of it, knew and loved its history and tradition, whose mum was a cleaner there. To know the deep love and passion Johan Cruyff felt for his only team serves to magnify his decision to sign for Feyenoord. This love of Ajax was more than a professional arrangement; this was his team. This was a football club encrypted in his DNA. As soon as he could walk, then kick a ball, it was Ajax he wanted to play for. The club meant everything to him.

As a child, youth and adult, Ajax nurtured, raised and developed the player into a football superstar. Cruyff joined the club on his tenth birthday, in 1957, and stayed until 1973, returning in 1981 until 1983. It's difficult to contemplate the depth of Cruyff's emotional bond to the club, and makes more astonishing their decision, to discard him, in 1983. It's difficult to imagine the emotional distress and hurt this would have caused the player, who had won three consecutive European Cups for the side.

It is arguable that Ajax president Ton Harmsen and the board possibly made one of the worst decisions in Dutch football when they decided not to continue with Cruyff's gate-deal pension fund arrangement for another year. To them, he had served his purpose. It was time for a sweeping change. Fans love a gesture; a strong president and board putting the club legend in his place. Cruyff was yesterday's man, a washed-up has-been. He was 36, but equally, he'd played a major part in securing the Eredivisie and the Dutch Cup for Ajax, so the decision came as a surprise, particularly to Cruyff.

Seldom in football has a club let an asset go only to see the decision rebound so spectacularly. Perhaps AC Milan's bizarre decision to let Andrea Pirlo run his contract down and then dump the playmaker, aged 32, after a decade, is comparable. Pirlo, deemed surplus to requirements by Massimiliano Allegri, went on to join Juventus and became a pivotal part of Antonio Conte's project to rouse the sleeping giant and help them win the league for the first time in nine years.

As a child, Cruyff grew up in the shadows of the Ajax De Meer Stadion, and his parents owned a greengrocer's shop in Betondorp. This was a working-class region, built after the First World War, and like many similar projects in cities across Europe, it was a social housing area. The Dutch had run out of bricks so started experimenting with low-cost pouring techniques with various types of concrete. Thus came the name Betondorp, which means *'Concrete Village'*, an architectural style best described on those BBC4 shows, as 'brutalist'.

Cruyff rarely complained though, and like most of his generation was allowed, even encouraged to play outside for hours on end. One of Cruyff's favourite mantras was 'turning a disadvantage into an advantage'. He claimed the concrete surroundings did not hinder his game but helped develop it. He would use the speed and strange angles the ball deflected off concrete surfaces, kerbs and walls to develop, turn and react to control it. He added, with the most profound logic, that playing on the concrete streets of Betondorp helped his balance on the ball, allowing him to stay on his feet as much as possible as it hurt when he fell on concrete.

When an Ajax player was out either injured or sick and unable to play and so receive a bonus (they were semi-professional and it was the 1950s), a young Johan would help his dad, who ran a fruit and veg stall, deliver baskets of fruit and vegetables to the stadium for the players. The staff at the club got to know Joppie, the 'delivery boy'. His dad's best friend, 'Uncle Henke', who worked at the club, allowed him to do odd jobs around the stadium.

One of Cruyff's earliest Ajax memories as a youngster was an evening match when he was on the pitch, under floodlights, in front of a full crowd. It wasn't to play though. Henke had arranged for him to help aerate the goal area at half-time with a pitchfork. Later, when Cruyff set up his foundation, he claimed this night had a lasting impact on him. It made him realise the importance of everyone involved at a football club, from the first team to the tea lady, to the cleaners, to the kit man, to the groundsmen who took such a pride in their roles. He would demand these high standards as a coach, pushing everyone to do their best, no matter the task.

One of Cruyff's heroes growing up was Dutch player Servaas 'Fass' Wilkes. When you watch grainy footage of Wilkes it's clear why. His game was based around creativity, dribbling, attacking and of course, scoring goals; a style of game very similar to Cruyff's. They both used individual skill, taking the ball around people with ease, and if there were any problems both had a great sprint to get away from tackles. Then there were the goals. Wilkes even had a habit of entertaining the crowds by keeping the ball when a simple pass was on. He appeared to skip and dodge tackles and like Cruyff, was an agile, elegant forward who could hold on to the ball under great pressure. The similarities are uncanny.

Wilkes signed for his local Rotterdam side, Xerxes, in 1940. His scoring exploits and attacking flair eventually earned a call-up to the Netherlands squad in 1946. On his debut, he scored four against Luxembourg, then scored a hat-trick against Belgium. Professional sides wanted to sign him but were blocked by the KNVB (Koninklijke Nederlandse Voetbalbond), the Royal Netherlands Football Association, for breaking its strictly amateur code. Wilkes remained determined to become professional. He eventually signed for Inter Milan in the summer of 1949. The KNVB was enraged and its chairman, Karel Lotsy, determined to preserve the amateur status of the game, imposed a five-year ban on Wilkes. You can see why

Cruyff described him as his idol, clearly not only for his skill as a player but someone strong-willed, who knew his mind and stood up to officialdom. Even back then the Dutch authorities clipped the wings of their best player. Maybe they didn't like anyone getting above their station?

It seems ludicrous that the KNVB would be so keen to impose and push these officious rules, to stop players like Wilkes from playing football for the national side, rather than trying to change the rules to allow him to appear. Before Cruyff, Wilkes was by far the best footballer the Dutch had ever produced; he earned 39 caps and scored 35 goals despite six years between 1949 and 1955 when he brought no end of disgrace on the KNVB by playing for Inter Milan and Torino in Italy, then in Spain with Valencia.

Young Johan had been hanging around and in and out of the De Meer Stadion from the age of five. So, by 15 November 1964, aged 17, when he made his debut for Ajax, nothing phased him. He scored in a 3-1 defeat to GVAV (the club became FC Groningen in 1971). His Ajax team-mates were more experienced and some had known him since he was a kid. They were able to keep his feet on the ground when he started getting mouthy. 'They were older. They would just guide me in the good things and the bad things and by the time I got to the first team, I wasn't nervous. It was all so natural, so automatic,' Cruyff once said.

The following season he scored his first hat-trick, 25 goals, and Ajax won the Eredivisie. When Cruyff had made his debut, Ajax weren't even the best side in Amsterdam. DWS (Door Wilskracht Sterk), who played home games at the Olympic

Stadium (Olympisch Stadion in Dutch), won the league that year. Until this point, Ajax were inefficiently run. Things would soon change when Jaap van Praag became president in 1964 and the following year, they hired Rinus Michels as coach.

Van Praag was an Ajax fan who started out working in his father's musical business but sensed there was future potential in the gramophone and record side, so branched out to open his own shop, called His Master's Voice. After the war, he continued to work in the music business. In the early 1960s, he presented a talent show, *Onbekend Talent* (Unknown Talent), a Dutch version of *Britain's Got Talent* for youngsters.

A lifelong Ajax fan, he became chairman in 1964. The club had been toiling, so along with financial help from his close friend, lifelong fan and investor Maup Caransa, a real estate developer, the club started to turn around. Then there was Leo Horn, a Dutch Jew who survived the German occupation. Horn was a textile factory owner who also hid Jews during the war and ambushed Nazi convoys. He had also invested in the club for years as well as providing paid work for Ajax players, who were still amateur before the Eredivisie came into play in the mid-1950s.

Van Praag spent most of the Second World War hiding above a photography shop in fear of persecution and being sent to the concentration camps. He made it through the war, but his family didn't. They were killed in Auschwitz. Van Praag's major backing and funding would come from an unexpected source, the brothers Freek and Wim Van der Meijden. The Van der Meijdens were building contractors and, during the war, their family business worked for the Germans, building barracks and gun positions during the Nazi occupation. They were Ajax fans and, wealthy from their previous enterprises, hoped by bankrolling the club they would be forgiven and win some influence. If you think that's a little weird, to add to the confusion, they would be joined on the board by Jaap Hordijk, who had played football for the Third Reich. It was strange but in the crazy world of football, it seemed to work. They backed Jaap van Praag, helping him achieve his lifelong ambition of becoming president, and provided the cash to bring in former Ajax striker Rinus Michels as a full-time coach, from Amsterdamesche FC.

When Michels, who by day was a PE teacher for deaf children, arrived in his battered Skoda in 1965, Ajax had just narrowly avoided relegation. When he strode into De Meer to replace Englishman Vic Buckingham, he had big plans for the ailing club. There was no fanfare and he was met with quiet indifference but Cruyff liked him. He immediately got the coach. He understood and shared his football philosophy and, surprisingly, despite disliking cross-country running, enjoyed his strict training and coaching regime, fitness and football tactics, and focus on technique and shape. They got on well and when Cruyff listened, he quickly realised he had someone who shared his football vision. Within six years, Michels and Cruyff would win the European Cup.

Ajax had been allowed to slide into mediocrity. They hadn't won a title since 1959/60, so when they started to get results under Michels, they were still regarded as whipper-snappers from east Amsterdam. They were in transition though. Van Praag moved the club away from one which was effectively run by people in their spare time and kept afloat by millionaire benefactors who would underwrite transfer fees and provide players with part-time jobs, to a more professional, forward-looking club. Before he arrived, most of the team worked, would train in the evenings and play at the weekend. Piet Keizer and Johan Cruyff were the only two full-time professionals.

Michels changed the approach, channelling the funding into a professional, well-run football club. Firstly, he cleared out the older players, then he trained the players hard, with shorter spells, more intense double shifts, sometimes twice a day. He then brought in a range of innovative ideas, well ahead of their time (at least for 1965) with advanced training equipment, and maintained a high level of discipline in the shape and attacking intent of the side.

Fitness was imperative but there would be more focus on technique and working with the ball. Piet Keizer, the wonderful left-footed winger, summed up Michels perfectly: 'When Michels took over, he changed the playing staff considerably, and changed the training even more. His was the hardest physical preparation I ever had. We sometimes had four sessions a day. He also introduced the Italian system of taking the players away for a period of concentrated training before a big match. We would start work in the morning and carry on until the evening.'

The players had to get used to a higher level of professionalism. Michels was a contradiction in terms. Here was a coach who believed in modern techniques with an innovative approach but was also resolute with time-honoured, established principles, like discipline and fitness. Most crucially though, he had a plan, and if the players did what was asked, collectively, they might carry it off.

He would attain results by maintaining a ruthless level of discipline. Keizer continued, 'He was by no means a miserable man, but he was very strict with the players and there were lots of arguments about discipline. The message was pretty clear; those who did not like it would have to leave.'

This football style was a boom time for Ajax and Cruyff, who could play anywhere and instantly understood what his coach required of him. They won the title in 1965/66 and did so again the following season, with Cruyff top scorer in the country, netting 33 goals. Another eight years would pass before their style of play would be christened, and given the name 'Total Football'.

Ajax and Netherlands legend Ruud Krol, who played for the club from 1968 to 1980, accurately explained what it meant as a defender to play this system: 'Michels made us run less and take over each other's positions, which was revolutionary. It was the first time there was a different vision of football. Total Football spread all over the world. It was the only real change in football for almost 40 years. He stunned the world.'

In the European Cup campaign of 1966/67, Ajax announced themselves on the European stage when they defeated Liverpool. The first leg of this second-round tie was played in the Olympic Stadium in Amsterdam, on 7 December 1966. The game was perilously close to being called off because the fog was so bad – what's Dutch for pea-souper? The match was so bad it was given the title 'De Mistwedstrijd', 'the Fog Match'.

Ajax hammered Liverpool 5-1. They clearly could see through the thick fog, with their passing and moving, which was better than Liverpool's. Ajax passed and moved faster, and more accurately. Context is everything as Ajax then were an unknown quantity, Liverpool and Shankly were famous. In the previous year's competition, Liverpool had reached the semi-finals, beaten by eventual winners Inter Milan. This wasn't a David versus Goliath situation, this was a serious miscalculation from the normally canny Scot. Shankly had failed to prepare and grossly under-estimated the opposition. He had even quipped to the press, asking, 'Who are Ajax anyway? Are they named after a popular British cleaning product?' No doubt it was accompanied by much guffaws and hilarity from those waiting for a killer line for the following day's papers. After the first leg shocker, Shankly remained flippant, telling the press Liverpool would win the home leg 7-0. Many across the football world still believed they would. In the first encounter it was Ajax who had cleaned up.

In the build-up to that game, if proof were needed that football had moved on significantly in terms of sports science and organisation, Sjaak Swart's car broke down and Cruyff, Swaart and Barry Hulshoff had to get out and push it to make it in time for kick-off. Later, they would admit during the game, they spoke about how knackered they were because of the impromptu shove. They still won.

During the second leg, Cruyff confessed to loving the unique atmosphere of English football when playing in Liverpool. The atmosphere inside Anfield had a lasting effect on him. He scored twice in a 2-2 draw to put Ajax through.

Ajax had enthralled those present at Anfield – even Shankly was impressed – and after the game, the Scot visited the Ajax dressing room to congratulate the team on their win. Rinus Michels wasn't one to get carried away by the result. He could see where the weaknesses lay and would be proven correct. In the quarter-finals, his side were beaten by Dukla Prague. The problem? There was no case for the defence.

Cruyff had a special relationship with Michels. He was allowed more leeway, time to learn; football was a game of mistakes. You learn from eradicating those errors. Michels recognised Cruyff immediately understood his vision of how the game should be read and played. Football was primarily a game of space, shape and angles. It was vital for Michels to have someone like Cruyff on the pitch instructing and guiding the side. He was often referred to as his on-field lieutenant, able to quickly shape and organise his side. One of the features of Cruyff's game, apart from his ability, was his constant pointing and controlling of players on their positioning during the match and telling everyone where to stand. Starting position was everything; football and Michels's system of playing required this level of perfection and precision for it to work tactically.

His Ajax team-mate Barry Hulshoff (who passed away in February 2020) shared some insight on what it was like to share the pitch with Cruyff: 'We discussed space the whole time. Cruyff always talked about where people should run, where they should stand, where they should not be moving. It was all about making space and coming into space.'

The football world started to take notice of this guy playing for Ajax. Cruyff had started to make waves. A few seasons after breaking through he was catching the eye, and then there was the result against Liverpool which really saw his profile rising. Quick, elegant, skilful and intelligent, he was central to the brand of football Ajax played. The team's style clashed with the prevalent one of an era when games could get agricultural. They were about power, strength and tough tackling, played on surfaces resembling half-ploughed farmland. Even then, Cruyff was able to dribble around players, and with his rangy long legs, vault over opponents trying to hit him and avoid ruthless tackles by somehow managing to glide over what would be red-card challenges today.

* * *

Returning home from a remarkable footballing odyssey, Cruyff was still in great shape, better than even he expected, and by 1981 he was keeping fit and training with Ajax. He was also able to keep up and compete. Ajax offered him a deal in December 1981 so he re-signed and that season they won the Eredivisie. The following season he won the league and cup double and was back in form, playing delightful stuff. In fact, during this period of his career, he scored one of his most memorable goals. When taking a penalty in 1982 against Helmond Sport, he passed to Jesper Olsen who rolled the ball back for Cruyff to tap in. When asked about it after the game, Cruyff remarked, 'With Christmas coming up, it seemed like a nice idea to do it so people would have something to talk about.'

Over the original nine seasons he had spent in Amsterdam, Cruyff won six league titles, four KNVB Cups and three consecutive European Cups. He scored 190 goals in 240 games and was awarded the Ballon d'Or in 1971 and 1973. In his second stint at the club in the 1980s, over 18 months he won two titles and a Dutch Cup. With this in mind, it's difficult to understand Ajax's decision in 1983 to jettison Cruyff. They decided not to go along with his terms and renew his contract. They claimed he was past his best. Had a career of being over-opinionated, shouting at team-mates, coaches, club officials and everyone who couldn't maintain his exacting standards come home to roost? Surely he had done enough for the club to take a gamble on, even rewarding their most famous player with a final season to go out in style? Not with the board then in charge at Ajax. And what did happen tells you more about them than it does about Cruyff.

Cor Coster, his agent, liked to have a plan B. If Ajax would not meet his terms, then Feyenoord would. To say Cruyff's venture to Rotterdam, behind enemy lines, was a shock would be a colossal understatement. He joined the club's biggest rivals, and, initially, they didn't like him much at all. The attendance at his first game wasn't great, and those present weren't interested in his titles, trophies and awards. Cruyff was met with ambivalence from the majority of fans and abuse from the hardcore element of the support. He would have a major job on his hands turning around the animosity echoing around Feyenoord's De Kuip Stadion.

Chapter 2

Season 1983/84:
Matchdays 1–6

WHEN IT came to box office and performing, Cruyff knew from an early age that football was about entertaining the fans and sending them home happy. Even in this, his final season – he would turn 37 before it was over in 1984 – he appreciated that fans deserved to be entertained.

With the second-best player of the 20th century (Pelé had been named first in a major poll) on board, the Rotterdammers started well. They only lost one point, winning five and drawing one in their first six games. They scored 14 goals in the first three league fixtures. Most footage of this year shows Cruyff coaching and organising on the park. He was also known for doing this when he broke into the Ajax first team and was famed for annoying older pros in the dressing room by telling them what to do.

Cruyff was often referred to as the 'orchestra conductor' due to his ability to control the dynamic and the way he would assert his personality on a game. You could imagine him as a composer, making exacting demands of everyone in the room (or in Cruyff's case, on the pitch), who can't get their head around or understand and play the perfect move.

Frustration mixed with magical brilliance made him mercurial but sometimes his frustration spilt over and inevitably got in the way. He was the first player representing his country to receive a red card. Cruyff was sent off playing in only his second international game against Czechoslovakia in 1967. The dismissal caused outrage and escalated into a huge national issue. The referee became irritated at Cruyff's incessant complaining about the hammering and kicking from opponents every time he received the ball. Cruyff was being kicked black and blue by the Czech side, who recognised he was the playmaker and targeted him. When he complained, the referee told him to keep his mouth shut.

When he received a blatant kick under the referee's nose, Cruyff approached again and demanded to know why the Czechs were allowed to behave this way and not be sanctioned. Instead, it was Cruyff who received the red card, and he was then banned from playing for his country for a year. Cruyff turned it into something more contemptuous, claiming it was cultural and political.

For him, it was proof if it were needed, that the world was changing, and changing quickly. This was about expression, freedom and how he, as part of the younger generation, represented something the older referee didn't like. This was 1967. The game was trying its best to evolve and modernise, but the referee remained rigid. 'The ref was the boss and no one questioned his authority and that is without mentioning the huge social difference between me, a young Western sportsperson in the age of Beatlemania and an East German who has to rule the field once a week for 90 minutes and then go back to keeping his trap shut in the GDR,' he later said. Cruyff was subtle, even then.

Cruyff seemed more mellow at Feyenoord, more patient and relaxed, but still, that determination was visible in games. This valedictory season would have been an exciting time for Dutch football, especially for smaller Eredivisie sides when the Cruyff circus came to town. He had been there before, playing for Ajax. They would be used to seeing the Dutch superstar but not in a Feyenoord shirt, surrounded by a phalanx of press, media and cameras.

With three decades of football experience, Cruyff knew the importance of the dressing room dynamic. Football is a team game, a squad of varying personalities and natures, some quiet, some boisterous. Many big-name players have waltzed into the dressing room, misjudged their self-importance and suddenly there's a revolt. How would the Feyenoord players handle an ageing football legend coming to their club? He was still a big enough star to not have a standard player contract like them. He had a box office deal and was identifiable just by one name, like musical superstars such as Sinatra and Elvis. Not only was he 'Cruyff', the icon of Dutch football, but to the players who supported Feyenoord he was 'Mr Ajax' and had switched allegiances. What was he even doing there? Cruyff got over that quickly. They liked what he was about and they appeared to buy into it.

Cruyff knew the dressing room had to be won over. No matter his status, he had to win his colleagues' respect, be funny, join in and he especially didn't want them thinking he was a washed-up pro, looking to make a final killing, masquerading as a team-mate. It was crucial that he struck the correct balance, proved himself to the older, more cynical guys in the dressing room and helped bring on the younger ones. If that worked, the fans would eventually follow.

Feyenoord had great players, including an established, consistent goalscorer in Peter Houtman, who in one of his many spells at the club, from 1982–85, scored 72 league goals in 96 games. He played eight times for the Netherlands and scored seven times. He remains a familiar face – and voice – around the club and has been Feyenoord's stadium announcer since 1998. There was also the emerging raw talent of Ruud Gullit and the free-scoring André Hoekstra in midfield. A great goalkeeper in Joop Heile and in front of him in defence, internationals Ben Wijnstekers (36 caps), Sjaak Troost (four) and Michel van de Korput (23). At left-back, they had Stanley Brard, who would eventually become head of the Feyenoord Football Academy. Their two foreign players, Denmark's Ivan Nielsen and Bulgaria's Andrey Zhelyaskov, were both internationals. Cruyff was not joining a team of rookies.

Gullit knew he was fortunate to share the park with Cruyff and used every second playing or training to learn from him, 'He was a leader and innovator. I played with him for a year at Feyenoord, he came to us, at 36. He came to Feyenoord for revenge after they treated him badly at Ajax, his own team, and said, "Okay, I'm going to show you." In training, I couldn't get the ball off him, at 36. He was so bony and it hurt when you tackled him. He would hit you with an elbow. He was so quick at the first five yards.'

In his first season as a pro at Haarlem, Gullit played at centre-half. The Welsh-born coach Barry Hughes encouraged him to go forward. He had the pace and power, a modern player, and scored 32 goals in 91 league appearances. In his second season there, under new coach Hans van Doorneveld, he played at centre-forward, adapted and scored regularly. Feyenoord came in for him and he still had some freedom but was playing on the right. When he made the move he caught the eye; you could see he was destined for far greater things. He played higher up the pitch. Cruyff knew he had the ability but needed some work on his tactical awareness. Gullit said, 'I had the opportunity to be with him and he was teaching me how to tactically play the game. He said you can play but I needed to learn how to play the game tactically. I learned a lot from him and I'm glad I had the opportunity to be there.'

Saturday, 20 August 1983. The beginning of 34 games in the Eredivisie. Each one a test of the ambition shown by the directors of Feyenoord in the brilliant but ageing superstar, Johan Cruyff. Coach Thijs Libregts and his side set off on their odyssey for their first league title since 1973/74.

Matchday one and Feyenoord travelled to FC Volendam. A crowd of 17,000 spectators showed up to witness the most famous player in the history of Dutch football secure a 4-1 victory for the visitors. Hopefully there wasn't too much bad language as Volendam is a pious, Catholic village; the original club was set up by local fishermen.

André Hoekstra started as he meant to go on for the season, opening the scoring after three minutes. Peter Houtman struck in the 25th and 38th minutes for a first-half double. Andrey Zhelyaskov made it 4-0 seven minutes into the second half. The home side managed a consolation goal when John Holshuijsen scored on the hour.

Matchdays two and three saw the first of two back-to-back home fixtures. Both games ended in the same 5-2 scoreline. A larger than usual crowd of 26,500 showed up to hurl abuse and wave banners at Cruyff. While there, they also witnessed some history; Cruyff's home league debut for Feyenoord over Helmond Sport.

Helmond hadn't read the script, taking the lead after Harry Lubse scored seven minutes into the game. It took an own goal from Jean-Pierre Andries before half-time to level the game.

I'm not sure what the Dutch for 'rocket' or 'hair-dryer' or 'throwing tea-cups' is but whatever Libregts launched at his men, it worked for the second half. Zhelyaskov scored in the 46th minute and Cruyff scored his first league goal for Feyenoord, the third of the game, three minutes later. Peter Corbijn pulled one back in the 60th minute before Zhelyaskov and Houtman wrapped it up at 5-2.

For their third league game, Feyenoord welcomed Fortuna Sittard. Huub Smeets put the visitors ahead in the second minute before Hoekstra equalised on the stroke of half-time. Zhelyaskov gave the home side the lead after 52 minutes and four minutes later Pierre Vermeulen made it three. Gullit scored on the hour to make it 4-1. Smeets scored his second goal of the game before Mario Been made it 5-2 in the 90th minute. The crowd of 24,090 headed home happy, and the vitriol toward Cruyff seemed to subside especially when the home support saw his team-mates celebrate with him.

On matchday four the Rotterdammers faced their first serious challenge when they headed to s' Hertogenbosch (The Duke's Forest) named after Henry I of Brabant, to face Den Bosch. Some 25,000 packed into the stadium, and the place rocked when the home side took the lead through Wim van der Horst. After breaking through the middle, he hit a great shot with the outside of his right foot and when the ball rebounded off the post, it fell kindly for the skilful midfielder to score. Cruyff equalised with a clever, first-time shot, accurately placed into the top corner. Cruyff received the ball from Hoekstra, in a central position, outside the 18-yard box. Before anyone had a chance to cover him, he had scored. It was the team's first dropped point but they were still unbeaten, the game finishing in a 1-1 draw.

For matchday five, Feyenoord travelled to the capital of the province of North Holland to face Haarlem. The city has a rich history, dating back to the middle ages. Haarlem is 12km north of Amsterdam, based on the thin strip of Netherlands at the top, and the city made its money initially from tolls on those ships and travellers crossing through from north and south. They are famed for their tulip growing. As shipping became more important, the capital moved to Amsterdam. A bumper crowd for Haarlem, 7,000, paid to see Feyenoord come to town. A Houtman goal in the 69th minute earned the win for the visitors.

On matchday six, Feyenoord faced Groningen at home, and a crowd of 25,889 showed up to see for themselves if something was maybe starting to happen.

This is football though and players are pack animals. It's about personalities and human nature. If there was any ill-feeling or jealousy, for example, over the amount Cruyff was paid, which would increase as crowds improved, you couldn't see it in the games. They were together, playing as a unit.

Cruyff coached while he played but he also dug in, and when he did anything spectacular it usually had an end product. Against Groningen, they won 2-0 with goals from Henk Duut and Hoekstra – somewhat ominously for Feyenoord though, Cruyff was substituted with what looked like a knock or a possible dead leg, early in the second half. Those from the club, fans and staff, even those reluctant at first, would be hoping it wasn't too serious. They were starting to see their team play with exuberance and confidence and Cruyff was the catalyst.

Could the Dutch Master be making such a difference? Their coach Thijs Libregts was confident the project would work, telling *De Telegraaf* he and Cruyff had a great understanding, and Cruyff's mentality and influence were exactly what his side needed, a clear voice on the pitch. Anyone watching the games could see Cruyff was doing everything possible, including marshalling senior pros into his way of playing. It looked like Cruyff was the player-coach, such was his input.

Feyenoord played with fluidity and shape and looked like they were enjoying their football. You wouldn't think, at this level, any professional footballer would see anything negative in a player of Cruyff's quality coming into the side. Maybe those who were dropped would take exception but you'd think they would try harder and want to be part of something. Younger players could learn a career's worth of advice from training with him every day and older players could prolong their careers. Imagine a world-class footballer coming into the side. What difference does it make if he's 36?

Chapter 3

Feyenoord Forever Cruyff Never

CRUYFF'S RETURN home from the USA to Amsterdam was initially quite accidental and natural. It was assumed he was at Ajax to get fit and keep in shape. He had been there as a technical adviser and it was, by Cruyff's standards, a low-key and perfectly sensible move, possibly into coaching. But it became a huge story when he signed to play in December 1981.

With Cruyff fit, refreshed, and in great form, the fans flocked for the return of the prodigal son. Gates were up and the side started to win, playing attacking and entertaining football. Cruyff was box office again and, knowing his pull and fame, his agent Cor Coster devised a clever plan with Ajax. Any income brought in above their average home gate would be halved between the club and Cruyff. The cash would go into Cruyff's pension fund. At this time, Dutch players still had a cap on their wage; their game was based on a low wage/high bonus system. Anything they earned above the cap was allowed to be paid into a pension, which they could access when they turned 40.

The arrangement was great for Cruyff and suited the club. All seemed well, at first, but this is football. The board started to get twitchy when they realised how much the gate plan yielded, and by the end of the 1982/83 season they had a change of heart. Most games were played at De Meer but when Ajax played in European ties, or bigger matches, they were moved to the Olympic Stadium. Fixtures against PSV could attract 35,000 and against Feyenoord 62,000, and according to Cruyff, many of the club's directors were resentful when they realised how much was transferred into his retirement pot, 'That season was very positive in every respect but one: the board decided that I was earning too much money.'

Cruyff held on to see what Ajax were going to offer. They procrastinated as they thought his earnings were too high through the lucrative crowd-based arrangement. When Coster and Cruyff countered that the board were also doing well, with the attendances up significantly because of Cruyff, they soon got to the crux of the matter. The board were angered at being tied to the gate deal plan and staggered at the hefty remuneration they were having to pay Cruyff. When it came to discussing his deal or extending, they told Cruyff he was no longer box office or attracting the same numbers through the turnstiles. The management started to discredit him, claimed he was too slow, had put on weight, and deliberately forced him out by offering a standard contract only, and not the deal he expected.

Football can be cruel. Even the greats are made to suffer. The narrative which has always been put out there is Ajax rejected Cruyff and reneged on a contract. They didn't. However, they deliberately forced Cruyff's hand, perhaps attempting to embarrass the player, hoping, and knowing, he would not accept the standard contract and they could stop the massive gate payments. It could be true that they had decided he was past his best and despite everything he gave the club, he was no longer of any use, aged 36. But Cruyff felt the hiatus in the US had extended his career.

The time might have been right, therefore, to go back and speak to Feyenoord. Cor Coster had established great contacts at De Kuip, and they had speculatively suggested if the Amsterdammers were having second thoughts or playing hardball, they would be willing to match a similar gate-based deal. When the insults started flying, and it became clear Ajax didn't want Cruyff, Feyenoord's proposal came back into the mix. Initially, the proposal might have been filed away under 'audacious'. Cruyff couldn't ever sign for Feyenoord. Then when they broke it down, he thought why not? It would be a challenge. Who were Ajax to treat a legend so shabbily? Feyenoord's stadium was bigger and held 47,000.

Cruyff clarified the whole saga in *My Turn,* when he explained, in detail, 'At the end of the 1982/83 season, I signed for Feyenoord, Ajax was still my team, but the people running it [Ajax] refused to go along with me. I heard they were saying I was too old and too fat and still putting on weight. I had to deal with all their objections. And they also demanded that I should be satisfied with a normal salary and of course, I wasn't.' With that, Cruyff's pride and sense of wrongdoing took him to Rotterdam.

There is a deep historical rivalry between both cities. I grew up thinking the Dutch were cool and kind of left of centre, what's not to love about the Dutch? They are a country of 17 million people and have 18 million bikes. I always assumed, until I took a serious interest in football, that most cities in the Netherlands got on with each other. I was wrong. This enmity isn't a recent issue. It's deep-seated and stretches back as far as the 14th century when both Amsterdam and Rotterdam were granted city status.

To over-simplify what is a complex cultural and historic issue in the Netherlands, the Dutch have a saying, 'Amsterdam to party, Den Haag to live and Rotterdam to work.' Amsterdam is generally regarded as the debauched, liberal, free-wheeling partying city; The Hague a beautiful, peaceful place to live and Rotterdam the austere, more serious working-class city. After Rotterdam was badly bombed during the Second World War, the city and its people recovered and started to enjoy life more. The teams are only 43 miles apart, yet there seems a cavernous divide between them. This is socio-political and cultural. Rotterdam is a port city – the second biggest in the world – a labour stronghold, hard-working. Amsterdam is the cosmopolitan, more philosophical, wealthier, artistic, liberal city.

Ajax are considered arrogant. It was often suggested they didn't care much about Feyenoord, or that the Rotterdam side hated them. Ajax didn't care what anyone thought about them, and this angered Feyenoord even more. Feyenoord fans are far more fervent, passionate and quick to anger. I have seen Ajax fans close up, in action, and I disagree with that. They aren't entirely made up of philosophers and artists.

The over-simplified consensus is that Ajax fans in the main, not their hardcore element, are broadly regarded as being over-indulged, used to success and quick to react when they aren't winning by not showing up. If the side aren't doing it on the pitch, they stay away. Feyenoord fans tend to thrive when they aren't doing well and will consistently turn up and deliberately be nice out of badness. Either way, there's a real nastiness between the fans, and there is something about this clash that brings out the worst in them both.

The players aren't any better. They bought into it too. Ajax legend Ruud Krol was none too subtle about how he felt while facing Feyenoord and going toe-to-toe in title races and vying for European Cup titles in the 1970s: 'We wanted to kill them.' You could say it was intense and vicious. It was more than a geographical generalisation. This had been passed down through generations.

The atmosphere between Feyenoord and Ajax fans was always partisan, divisive and prone to exploding. Any excuse for a riot. We cannot skirt around the elephant in the room. These fans hate each other. In 1997, the hooligan element from both sides showed up for a deliberately organised, pre-arranged battle. The call to arms, or greeting, involved attacking each other with knives, hammers, and bats, anything they could get a hold of. The Battle of Beverwik saw a man killed. Hooliganism elevated to murder. That's the level of organised violence off the pitch.

Even the first 'De Klassieker' played between *De Trots van Zuid* (The Pride of the South) Feyenoord, and *De Godenzonen* (Sons of the Gods) Ajax, on 9 October 1921, was mired in controversy and bordered on farce. The game finished 3-2 to the visitors, Ajax. Feyenoord launched a protest claiming Ajax's winning goal was 'dubious'. I'm not sure what the 1920s Dutch equivalent of VAR would be, but this particular dubious goals committee decided that the goal was indeed dubious. We need more. What happened? Was it offside? A handball? Anyway, their winning goal was over-ruled. The points were eventually shared and in truth, both sides haven't ever fully recovered from that.

What is certain about the origins of Dutch football and this era, is that the game was elitist. It was run by the aristocracy, the wealthy, and they liked it that way. It wasn't played by the poor, only the rich. Those running it would decide who would become members. It was like a snobbish golf, rowing or cricket club, and the poor were kept out. None of the 'people's game' nonsense for these founding fathers. The poor were too busy working to play games anyway. By 1908, a side called Wilhelmina were formed and in 1912, changed their name to Rotterdamsche Voetbal Vereeniging Feijenoord (Rotterdam Football Club Feijenoord). They were from the south of Rotterdam, an industrial working-class area, the docks providing many with work.

The working men's club rapidly improved, and within a few years were soon mixing it with the gentlemen's clubs who were used to having it their own way. So, with that brief history lesson, let me interject an idea. Ajax may have been scared of the power, or popularity and fervour of the working-class side from the south. Feyenoord decided to appeal because Ajax may have behaved like most public schoolboys and were dastardly cheats anyway. Just a thought, mostly from a Jeeves and Wooster, Fleishman and Alf Tupper point of view.

By 1983, Feyenoord had toiled and struggled as lesser sides overtook them. Feyenoord were the first Dutch team to win the European Cup, beating Celtic in the 1970 final, in Milan. But by the early 1980s the feeling among Dutch football fans was even Feyenoord weren't Feyenoord anymore. They were now another big city side who had struggled and hadn't won a league title since 1974. Clubs like PSV Eindhoven and AZ Alkmaar had joined the party. Some of their form in the seasons before Cruyff's arrival was poor to average. In 1979/80, 1980/81 and 1981/82 they finished fourth, fourth and sixth respectively.

Cruyff's move to Feyenoord could be compared in the modern era to Messi signing for Real Madrid, or more realistically, in pure football terms, Mo Salah leaving Liverpool to sign for a struggling Manchester United, toiling around fifth or sixth, winning the league and cup double, and being named player of the year. (For clarity, the Dutch Player of the Year is the Dutch Football Association's award and is voted for by fellow professionals from the top two divisions. This was won by Ruud Gullit. There was also an award voted by influential newspaper *De Telegraaf* and football magazine *Voetbal International*, a prestigious press award called the Gouden Schoen, the Golden Boot, which Cruyff won).

Footage of Cruyff signing for Feyenoord is still difficult viewing. A psychiatrist would have a field day as the chairman, Gerard Kerkum, nervously and coldly speaks to the press as Cruyff sits awkwardly, waiting for a pen. Feyenoord coach Thijs Libregts looks like he's waiting on a bus to take him to the dentist for root canal surgery.

Perhaps the fear had set in as the chairman pondered over the deal and wondered why they had even considered making any kind of approach to Cruyff. What if there was another coup? Maybe they remembered the first time he left Ajax. Cruyff had constantly placed demands on his team-mates despite not being a coach, so they revolted, stripped him of his captaincy, and Cruyff, feeling betrayed, headed to Barcelona.

Why had Cruyff accepted the offer from Feyenoord? Had anyone considered the prospect of how much this could go wrong? From Cruyff's perspective, he would be thinking about the time Ajax were holding out and determined to sell him to Real Madrid. He threatened to quit if they didn't sell him to the Catalans. This was well before player power; Cruyff knew his worth and his own mind. He was older in 1983 and his move to Feyenoord might have been difficult – but he knew he could do it.

The natives were already restless and slightly confused with it all. For home games, attendances weren't improving as much as expected, initially only increasing by two or three thousand. The away fixtures though had all sold out.

Cruyff knew what he had to do when he played his first game for Feyenoord. He had to win the fans over. He understood he was the bad guy, 'I had to convince the fans of my loyalty and make sure that we won. Just as I did at Barcelona, the Los Angeles Aztecs, Washington Diplomats and Ajax, I managed to win them over during my first match. I scored a great goal in what was then the Rotterdam Tournament. Everyone started cheering. Then they suddenly seemed to realise they were cheering for someone they hated. For a moment the whole stadium was in a state of total confusion but the ice was broken when they saw how happy my team-mates were. To round everything off nicely, we went on to win the tournament.'

However, when he played his first home game at De Kuip, in front of the hardcore Feyenoord fans, it was different. The supporters who attend league games don't tend to enjoy family-friendly competitions and invitational pre-season tournaments. There's less chance of a fight for a start. In the first league game, fans had placed banners out to let Cruyff know, in no uncertain terms, what they truly thought of him. One of the few polite ones read 'Feyenoord Forever Cruyff Never'. Another advised 'Cruyff Get Lost', while others were more stark with their advice and instruction to the board and player, in language more befitting of the docks. News footage of the time had images of the hardcore fans unhappy as they ripped up season tickets for the cameras.

Cruyff's main concerns were his fitness and age. He was an experienced athlete who had played for over three decades and knew his body. He may also have considered the period between 1979 and 1981, with the time off, moving to America, briefly helping at Ajax, then Levante, as an extended break with games as paid exercise. Cruyff would know that this period and then playing at a lower standard in America had bought his career at least another few years.

It was still a colossal gamble for both Feyenoord and Cruyff. However, the fans and board of the club had failed to factor in one crucial component. They didn't understand the depth of Cruyff's ferocity and vindictiveness at what he saw as an act of betrayal. He wasn't even driven by money now, but a determination to prove Ajax wrong for daring to assume he was finished.

Chapter 4

Season 1983/84: Matchday 7
De Klassieker: 8-2 Defeat and Cruyff
'We Will Win the Championship'

THE DAY had finally arrived. An Ajax legend, one of the most important players to ever have played for the side, who had supported the club since an infant, played in their youth system from the age of ten, and who would go on to win three European Cups, was back in the shirt of their adversaries. The first of this season's matches against Ajax took place in the Olympic Stadium on 18 September 1983. How surreal an afternoon must this have been for Johan Cruyff?

Feyenoord would have faced Ajax with both optimism and caution; they hadn't truly been tested in their opening six matches. However, they headed into the game with Gullit and Houtman in great form and of course, a midfielder going by the name of Cruyff with something of a point to prove. Scribes prepared themselves for an epic honk on their cliché horn and dusted down the most obvious and repeated cliché in football: in these games, the form book goes out of the window.

The focus in the build-up in Rotterdam, the Netherlands and around the world was how Cruyff would handle the occasion. Everyone knew he was an Ajax fan as well as a former club legend. Would he be able to handle the crowd? How would they react to him? How would he react in the highly probable scenario in which he might score? Would someone who everyone knew was one of the toughest psychologically be able to deal with coming back to his spiritual home? The media circus burst into overdrive as the game kicked off. In the following 90 minutes, Cruyff hardly featured in the unfolding drama.

Cruyff had to settle for second billing in a wet and strange De Klassieker, behind the final score: an 8-2 defeat. Feyenoord started on the back foot while Ajax pressed. Slack and careless defending would eventually lead to the opening goal as Jesper Olsen was allowed to come in from a wide position and wait for the inevitable gap to open up before hitting a great left-footed shot into the net. Five minutes gone and already 1-0 down, caught with a sucker punch, Feyenoord should've been shaken out of their slumbers and slapped back into reality. They should've tightened up, tried to get organised and find their feet.

In the 14th minute, Marco van Basten was given the freedom of Amsterdam from a corner and was allowed to rattle in the second goal. He looked in the mood from the start. Hardly any sign yet of Cruyff, so sportswriters may have been double-checking their team sheets to make sure he hadn't pulled a hamstring in the warm-up and was still playing.

Ajax thrived in the wet conditions. Olsen drove at the Feyenoord defence and put in Peter Boeve who scored the third, finishing excellently with a left-footed shot after 24 minutes. Cruyff's return was beginning to look chaotic. Perhaps Feyenoord should consider parking the bus? Find a second wind, consolidate, go longer than eight minutes without conceding another goal. Could one of those mental-looking defenders, like Stafleu, take a yellow for going through Olsen or van Basten?

As you can imagine, the home fans enjoyed every second as they witnessed Feyenoord struggle and unravel. It looked and sounded like party time around the ground. Sights of the most iconic player the Netherlands had ever produced were rare. And when he was spotted, Cruyff looked his age during the game, off the pace and not his usual self.

When Gullit drove forward on the right and cut back to Houtman who opened his body up to meet and thunder home a right-foot shot after 27 minutes, the Rotterdammers pulled one back. Feyenoord played their way back into the game and six minutes later, when the ball came in from the right, Ajax failed to clear their lines and Houtman cut it back to Henk Duut for a left-footed strike to make it 3-2.

When Olsen swung in a corner, Keje Molenaar leapt above what looked like four Feyenoord defenders hanging around waiting for a tram. They should've been trying to mark Molenaar who met it with a high, looping header in the 61st minute to make it 4-2.

This game was strange. Despite the scoreline, even at this point, at 4-2, Feyenoord remained in the encounter. The goals they conceded were mostly self-inflicted and caused by basic errors. Ajax were clinical on the counter attack, slick in the pass and deadly with their finishing.

When Olsen again seized upon slackness from a Feyenoord high line, he quickly darted away, veering down the left and Michel van de Korput did well to catch him but brought the flying Dane down in the box with a late slide tackle. Ronald Koeman dispatched the resulting penalty to make it 5-2. There were still at least 30 minutes more to come and van Basten was later put through for his second in the 75th minute and expertly slotted home with a wonderful left-foot shot from 18 yards.

As you watch the game, you wonder if Feyenoord had a bout of food poisoning. After 84 minutes, again, the point about errors was highlighted. Olsen seized on some uncertainty from Hoekstra in the Ajax box – as the Feyenoord midfielder failed to capitalise, his hesitancy was seized upon. The ball was played to van Basten who picked it up deep, played a delightful through ball, and Olsen checked inside for a perfect finish.

Van Basten made it 8-2 and completed his hat-trick with three minutes remaining. He showed more desire to win possession, drove through, remained calm and delightfully chipped the ball over the keeper.

Again, it's a strange thing to suggest but Feyenoord didn't play badly. They started poorly and defended terribly but at one point came back into the game. Tactically, Ajax caught Feyenoord on the counter attack for many of the goals. Feyenoord looked like they were playing five at the back with a 5-3-2 system but Ajax shaped up in a 4-4-2 and looked as if they had a spare midfielder every time they broke into Feyenoord's half. And Cruyff was largely absent from the game. Along with the ten goals, there was the obligatory crowd trouble.

The punters had shown up to see Cruyff but a wonderful double act performance from van Basten and Olsen stole the show. It would have been interesting to hear if Cruyff spoke to any of his old team-mates, especially van Basten. As Rinus Michels was to Cruyff's development and sharing of tactics, Cruyff was to van Basten (later, as Barcelona coach, he would mentor Pep Guardiola in the same way). Eighteen-year-old van Basten had played with the same talent, technique and discipline driven into him and everyone who came through the Ajax system. In this performance he confirmed, at that time at least, he was on his way to becoming a world-class player.

This game would turn out to be a decisive moment; an incident that led to the player turning a disadvantage to an advantage. After this shocking humiliation, Cruyff went around the dressing room and told them not to worry. He said they would now go on and win the title. The older pros in the team must've looked at him with some disdain and wondered what planet he was on.

For Cruyff's part, it may have been bravado or an attempt to rally and motivate the troops, but he also may have noticed something in the Ajax side and could see a weakness other sides would capitalise on throughout the season. Equally, he may have realised that there was something not right in the Feyenoord team and the result confirmed his fears. He had the influence and power to do something about it. It is difficult to remain philosophical after an 8-2 defeat to your bitter rivals. There were some self-inflicted errors, poor marking, and they may have been up against a side where everything seemed to fall perfectly. That aside, it must have been painful to hear the Ajax players' celebrations bouncing off the walls next door.

Cruyff might have been reminding them, in his own way, that as in life, as well as football, when a calamitous event occurs, nothing as bad can surely happen again. These situations should galvanise you, forcing you to make your own luck. Just to get his point across, he went on national TV in the Dutch highlights show and told millions of viewers, 'It was only two points, the prizes are given out at the end of the competition at the end of the 34 games, just wait. You'll see.'

Chapter 5

Betrayal, Brutal Coup
and Heading to Barca

CRUYFF'S CAREER was littered with explosive moments, arguments and confrontations. There were so many inciting incidents, plot lines and hints nudging us toward a climactic coda and to this final scene of his playing career, in 1983, and the near implausible move from Ajax to Feyenoord. His drive for perfection saw him clash with team-mates and coaches. One of the biggest calumnies, in Cruyff's head, occurred in August 1973.

After playing for Ajax for nine years, he fell out with his team-mates after a bloody coup to oust him as club captain. His team-mates had become sick of his incessant criticism and felt he needed to be cut down to size.

Shortly before he was overthrown, Cruyff had considered his future and assumed he would be remaining at Ajax to continue building his football legacy while also securing his family's future in Amsterdam. He had extended his contract for another seven years. They had won a third consecutive European Cup. He appeared happy and settled.

Ajax coach Ştefan Kovács left in the summer of 1973 and was replaced by George Knobel. Kovács, the pleasant Romanian, had won two of the club's three European Cups and moved on to become national coach of France.

Cruyff blamed the player unrest on Kovács and his coaching approach. There was a lack of discipline, and he described Kovács's style as 'hands off'. He had replaced the strict disciplinarian, Rinus Michels, who controlled the players and supervised the training. He was meticulous about detail. Kovács, on the other hand, preferred to let the players get on with it.

With Knobel now in charge, on a pre-season training camp, the players selected their captain for the following season. During a team meeting, it was decided there would be a ballot to see who would have the captaincy. The players picked Piet Keizer. Cruyff explained, in detail, in his autobiography, 'I'd just suggested staying on as captain when I heard that I had a rival candidate in Piet Keizer, so there was going to be a ballot. People were still complaining that I was too self-serving. It was a form of jealousy I had never before experienced.'

Cruyff as ever would read the situation differently, blaming Kovács for setting up the side and expecting the players to run the team. Cruyff thought he was simply applying the instructions and tactics his coach wanted from him. He also knew with so much power on the park, he might incur the wrath of his team-mates. Though why wouldn't any clever coach build a side around one of the best players in the world? Kovács set up the side and left it to Cruyff, who was a striker but when Total Football was correctly applied, he would be anywhere on the pitch.

Cruyff would be right. This was the ruthlessly nuanced backstabbing environment of the football dressing room. He was amazed the event even happened ahead of the season. Cruyff had spoken to the team and suggested he remained captain. Then there was a vote, Cruyff was ousted and Keizer was in. 'The blow was particularly severe as we weren't just fellow players but close friends,' he said.

The player would speak extensively over the years about his ousting at Ajax. It was another one of those where he turned the disadvantage into an advantage. He felt aggrieved, it wasn't his fault. The vote was unfair. This was a betrayal after everything he had done for them. He had been bullied and this decision was ill-thought through. Such was Cruyff's relentless drive for perfection, he may not even have realised he was undermining and annoying his Ajax team-mates.

In David Winner's *Brilliant Orange*, Johnny Rep doesn't pull any punches when discussing Cruyff's insistence on perfection, on talking incessantly, his nature and ego. He felt it was the reason why he lost that captaincy vote, 'It was not easy, not all the time. He said you must do this in a game, or you must do that. It was not easy for me to shut my mouth. He was always saying: more to the right, or to the left, or the centre. Always! If he gave a bad ball, it was not his fault. And he is always right! He is the best and all the time he is right. That was the problem with him for me.'

Cruyff was in shock. The incoming manager George Knobel should not have allowed it. Keizer won the vote with a significant majority. We seldom hear the players' side – apart from Rep's. 'We just wanted to take someone else,' recalled

Rep. 'But I think it broke something for Johan. That was it for him. We went further with Johan as a player. But the talking, it was terrible.'

Such was Cruyff's nature and mentality that when he felt wronged, he was compelled to react. He spoke to his agent and set in motion a move which would eventually lead him to Barcelona. When Cor Coster and Barcelona initiated negotiations for the Dutchman, he was, arguably, at this point, the most famous footballer in the world. Equally, at this time, the Catalan side was struggling, but Cruyff had many reasons to move there. He had been to the city on holiday, loved the area, the spirit of the city and the fact the club was such a central part of life there. His mentor, Rinus Michels, had moved there two years previously and shared a bond and an understanding of how the game should be played.

After the captaincy issue, Ajax knew Cruyff would be leaving, and hunkered down, determined to make any move as difficult as possible for the player. Ajax wanted him to sign for Real Madrid but Cruyff would not budge; he was set for Catalonia and would hold out at Ajax until he got the move. Cruyff knew his worth, was smart and used his player power strategically. They wanted him to accept the million-pound offer made by Real but Cruyff was determined it would be Barcelona. He waited, and won.

Cruyff had every reason to feel hurt. Not only had his friends ousted him as captain and his club prevented him leaving, but the Dutch football association, the KNVB, was also irate at him for turning his back on Ajax. The transfer window in the Netherlands ended in July but the Spanish window didn't close until August. When Cruyff moved to Barcelona, the KNVB acted to prevent him from playing, so he had to wait for two months before making his competitive debut.

With the Dutch playing a crucial World Cup qualifier against Belgium in November and with their friendly matches lined up, Cruyff threatened to withdraw from any of these games, putting his place in the Dutch squad for the 1974 finals in West Germany in jeopardy. He argued that if he wasn't allowed to play, he couldn't make himself available without match practice. Barcelona organised four friendly matches for the fans to see him and thankfully his protest, or veiled threat, worked. Again, he used his player power smartly, threatening to withdraw if he wasn't getting games in.

In the early 1970s, Spain had become so popular with holidaymakers that few cared or even bothered about domestic football. Tourists didn't care about the nation's politics and ignored the fascist dictatorship of General Franco; they didn't care about the Catalan or Basque people and their cultural identity being eroded and destroyed by a wicked regime. The destination was cheap, hot and easily accessible; a few hours away on a flight. Spain had morphed into a holiday spot mecca of sun, sea and sangria. It was not a destination for top football players or fans. That would soon change when Cruyff touched down in Barcelona.

So, when Cruyff fell out with his team-mates and the board at Ajax, there was only one destination he had in mind, and it wasn't Madrid. He made it clear he would not sign for any team who had links to Franco's regime. By this point, Franco's days of evil dictatorship had become passé; he was ill and frail.

Someone vibrant and fresh was on his way and coming to whip it up in Catalonia – a skinny guy with long legs from the land of windmills and a bit of lip. Rinus Michels had already been attempting to rebuild and shape his Barcelona side based around his football philosophy. When Cruyff joined him from Ajax, he became the crucial final piece of the jigsaw and the project clicked into place.

On 22 August 1973, it felt like the world had shown up to witness the most expensive footballer ever arrive at Barcelona Airport. The (sleeping) Catalan giants had reluctantly agreed to pay six million Dutch guilders (£929,000) for Cruyff. Barcelona would have been happy that they got the transfer over the line as they became nervous, especially when Ajax chairman Jaap van Praag held out for the bigger fee from Real Madrid. Barcelona had already started to shilly-shally and have second thoughts over the size of the fee. When they realised they would be paying a world-record sum of £929,000 for Cruyff, they became nervous. They only started to move when Real Madrid had offered a full million.

Cruyff was happy though, 'Two things are etched in my memory and have always stayed with me. First the huge crowd at the airport and the enormous hope and expectation for what I would do. It was overwhelming. Soccer here wasn't just a sport … but also a political affair. Soccer was an escape valve and something people could draw life from.'

You would be forgiven for thinking that Steve McQueen, Paul Newman and Elvis were arriving at the airport. But it was Cruyff, on a KLM flight. One thing strikes you amid the cauldron of noise, and the claustrophobic excitement as the player is manhandled by police, airport staff, fans, the press and camera crews, and that's his smile. Cruyff looks so happy. Even as the circus practically engulfs him, he is relaxed and laughing at it all.

In September 1973, Cruyff made his debut against Cercle Brugge, scoring a hat-trick in a 6-0 win. These friendlies were a huge success, pulling in large crowds with games against Kickers, Arsenal and Orense recouping the player's transfer fee. Barcelona won all four and gathered some much-needed impetus and momentum, which they then took into their abysmal league form. At this point, Barcelona had sunk to fourth from bottom of the league. Of their first seven games they had managed only to win two. They had also been knocked out of the UEFA Cup. The natives had become restless and many refused to show up to even watch their team. They needed a hero and Cruyff delivered.

The Dutch Master made his LaLiga debut, on 28 October 1973, at the Nou Camp against Granada CF. Barcelona won 4-0 and Cruyff scored twice. From then on, the team didn't lose until they won the league with eight points to spare (they lost a few times after the league was sealed). Cruyff learned quickly that the Catalans were a unique group of people, 'We then won LaLiga in 1973 without losing a single game. Here, winning the league was already pretty spectacular. What struck me was people didn't say congratulations, they said thank you. And from that moment on, you begin to understand the Catalan character. How they experience things.'

Drama is seldom exiled when Cruyff is involved and it seemed fitting that he would be fashionably late after the incompetent and some would say, deliberate procrastination of the authorities, but boy what a difference when he got the team going. Barcelona beat Sporting Gijon 5-1, Malaga 4-0 and Celta Vigo 5-2. They were ruthless as they fought their way up the league from 14th position on Cruyff's arrival in October, to move six clear at the top by the time they humiliated Real Madrid in February 1974.

There was little to no difference in the way Cruyff applied his system as a player or a manager. He had a clear, well-defined method of approach. When he arrived in Barcelona as a player, there was work to be done. Charly Rexach, who spent a total of 44 years at Barcelona as a player, youth coach, assistant manager and even caretaker manager, played in the same side as Cruyff and would later become his assistant manager. No one is better placed to explain the before and after, and Cruyff's influence on the side. This wasn't a tweaking or a few tactical changes, this was a radical overhaul – a complete change of approach. Rexach said, 'Back then football was, "Right, out we go: come on lads, in hard," and that was it. No one studied the opponents. It was fight, run, jump. Then it was, "No, let's play better football."'

Juan Manuel Asensi played at Barcelona from 1970 to 1980 and so remembered the transformation under the Dutchman. He noted Cruyff's enthusiasm and how it eventually became infectious, 'With Cruyff, everything changed – the club as well as the team.' He was fearless when it came to how he wanted football played and unafraid to stand up to anyone who would not buy into it. He would apply the same principles as a player and later as a coach, an approach which would constantly lead to friction with those running the club. It was seldom dull.

Around this time, before committing to Cruyff, Barca had another wish list with Gerd Müller's name on it. Müller came close to signing and seemed keen but the deal broke down. The Bayern Munich and West German superstar was a goalscoring machine with 68 goals in 62 international games, 66 goals in 74 European ties for Bayern, and a vast array and varying total (depending on the source) of 566 career goals in 607 games. He scored the winner in the World Cup Final against Cruyff and Michels's Dutch 'Total Football' side … Müller was one of those legendary footballers who provoked colossal levels of understatement from pundits who would say that 'he had a nose for goal' or 'he knew where the goals were'.

His superb goals-to-game ratio was derived from his balance, poise, power, athleticism, low centre of gravity and lightning quick instinct. Rinus Michels wanted him ahead of Cruyff. The deal fell through – at this point, Bayern were a far more successful club, having won three Bundesliga titles in succession between 1971 and 1973, then three European Cups from 1974 to 1976. With the following year's World Cup on home soil, Müller may have preferred Bavaria to Barcelona, and to remain at home in a side which would provide the nucleus of the world champions. In truth, Bayern were to Müller as Ajax were to Cruyff; when they joined their respective sides they were in the wilderness but both players brought extraordinary success.

Those with a fondness for football what-if accounts can only wonder what would've happened if Barcelona had broken the bank and signed both Cruyff and Gerd Müller. What a mouth-watering prospect for the neutral. Der Bomber hasn't had his struggles to seek. Bayern helped him in his fight with alcoholism, then in 2015, he was diagnosed with Alzheimer's disease. What a wonderful player, the perfect goalscorer; fast over five yards, brave and prolific.

Chapter 6

Best Match for Barcelona: at Bernabéu v Real Madrid, 1974

THIS EL Clásico was, in reality, just another two points for a league victory – but it was also so much more than that.

If anything, the Barcelona move energised Cruyff's game. Maybe it was as simple as a relaxing of tension, or the release of a fresh challenge, but whatever he was doing worked. The club hadn't won the league for 14 years and needed something, anything to turn it around.

When Cruyff joined Barca they were struggling in the league but after the first game against Granada, they didn't lose until the title was won.

Cruyff remained modest about playing for Barcelona, 'Barcelona had some good players but they didn't think like that. As soon as they started to believe again, they started to win again.' You also had a sense, for the Real Madrid game, that he planned to soak in and enjoy the experience, 'It was fantastic for me as a player to play Madrid. It was such a huge thing, first to play in the Bernabéu, then you saw the game, we played very well.'

During this period, from October 1973 to the end of the season and then rolling into the World Cup of 1974 in West Germany, for Barcelona and the Netherlands, Cruyff played the best football of his career. He also scored one of his best goals this year, against Atlético Madrid, when he leapt into the air and scored with a seemingly impossible right-footed back-heel volley, at full stretch, while facing away from the keeper, Miguel Reina. It became known as the 'phantom goal'. During this league run, he would play his best game for Barcelona.

Cruyff had left Amsterdam to play in Barcelona and galvanised both the Catalan people and the club, helping them to the title. If one game epitomised the relationship between Rinus Michels, Cruyff and the Barcelona faithful, it occurred on 17 February 1974, away to Real Madrid in the Bernabéu. Barcelona won 5-0.

As if to show his (or more accurately, his wife's) dedication to the cause, on the date of the game Danny was due to give birth by caesarean. Such was the importance of the encounter, Rinus Michels wanted Cruyff to change the date of the birth. Michels wanted his star in the correct frame of mind for the crucial El Clásico. Cruyff was a professional footballer and such occurrences could not get in the way of a big game. The player agreed and promised to look into the situation. He asked Danny, then everyone concerned from the hospital, and, amazingly, no one objected.

Subsequently, the date was brought forward by a week and their third child, Jordi, was born on 9 February. Cruyff would go on to star as Barcelona won convincingly. Meanwhile, Danny and her latest addition were still in Amsterdam, and not allowed to fly for ten days after the birth. Cruyff then flew to collect them from the hospital, and a few days later he headed back to Barcelona. Like his two sisters, Chantal and Susila, Jordi was born in Amsterdam and his birth was registered there.

When they returned, Catalonia was still celebrating the victory over Real Madrid. Suddenly, Cruyff was back in the heart of it and everywhere he looked, they continued to party. He realised how important it was to them, 'That result in the Bernabéu had an incredible impact, not just on the club, but also on the whole of Catalonia. The region was suffering under the tough regime of the dictator Franco in the capital so the victory had huge political significance.'

As required, he also had to register the birth in Spain. But the name Jordi was banned by Spanish authorities. Jordi was the patron saint of Catalonia. He even had a feast day, 23 April. Cruyff was told to come up with another name or change it to the Spanish version, Jorge. Cruyff held firm. They were Dutch, the family loved the name, and had discussed it for a while. Jordi was already registered in the Netherlands, and they were adamant that would be his name. On changing the name to the Spanish version, Cruyff explains, "Then we've got a problem then," I told the official. "His name is Jordi and Jordi it will remain. If you won't do it, then I will take it further but in that case, it will become your problem."' Jordi it was.

Cruyff would later explain that this was pivotal to his popularity in Barcelona, not only because of his time as a player and a coach but because he named his son after Catalonia's patron saint.

Everyone knew the bitterness between Real Madrid and Barcelona was as much about politics as football. So, when Cruyff rejected Madrid and held out for his Barca deal, the tension was even higher when he played in the five-goal trouncing at the Bernabéu. The game turned into a spectacular high point for Barcelona fans in a season that saw the title return to the Nou Camp for the first time since 1960. The Catalans saw the result as hugely symbolic and pivotal. Even then, people were being arrested and imprisoned for speaking in Catalan.

Cruyff hadn't only orchestrated a stunning Barcelona performance but in beating Real Madrid 5-0, Catalonia had kicked the federal government in the capital. If there had been any doubt the messiah had arrived, JC lived and walked among them. Cruyff was now the saviour of Catalonia. He said, 'After that 5-0 victory, we played a series of matches whose like had never been seen before. Three months later, Barcelona were national champions for the first time in 14 years. It was an unforgettable experience and one that still gives me a good feeling when I think back on it.'

Antonio de la Cruz played at Barcelona from 1972 to 1979. When it came to the cultural as well as political significance of the result, he was eloquent and clear, 'For those of us who were lucky enough to play in that team, we will remember that match forever … Things were beginning to change in Spain. People were starting to be able to say what they thought politically and in that sense, a result like that against a team like Real Madrid, in their ground, sent shockwaves around Europe.'

Madrid president Santiago Bernabéu had signed Günter Netzer from Borussia Mönchengladbach (the following season he would sign Paul Breitner from Bayern) to match Barcelona's signing of Cruyff. The build-up to the game focused on Cruyff and Netzer – but it was Cruyff who stole the show. The Dutch superstar was untouchable throughout and controlled the game, scoring an excellent goal and setting up another three.

On analysis of the result, several elements become evident. Firstly, the pitch is like a bowling green, in stark contrast to surfaces Cruyff would later be performing on ten years later at Ajax and Feyenoord. This also meant passes remained true; the movement of the ball is slick and fast. Secondly, Cruyff is the star, so much better than everyone else on the park. He plays with a tempo and confidence. He is also fouled regularly. Some of them are truly shocking tackles, and it needs repeating, by today's standard, referees would brandish a red. Cruyff appears used to it, gets up and plays on with no histrionics.

After 30 minutes, some clever wing play down the right side by Marcial lost Netzer, beating him to the byline to cut back for Asensi to score from close range. If he hadn't rattled it in, Cruyff waited behind him, primed and ready to do it. After 39 minutes, Hugo Alejandro Sotil Yerén, to his mum and dad, Sotil to us, picked up the ball in midfield. The wonderful Peruvian striker, who also played as an attacking midfielder, was a superstar in his homeland, nicknamed El Cholo and much loved because of the success he found from such a humble background. In Peru, in the 1970s, he was a great footballing hero, one of the country's most renowned players, along with Teófilo Cubillas and Héctor Chumpitaz.

Cruyff pointed to where he wanted it delivered and Sotil obliged, playing Cruyff in. Sotil continued his run, waiting for the ball back but Cruyff left three Madrid players standing when he dipped in the opposite direction, drove into the box and dodged tackles. The Real Madrid defence couldn't get the ball off him. It looked like he was dribbling around kids in the playground and no one could get near him, it was done so effortlessly. He was allowed to take it on his left and hit it low and hard to make it 2-0.

Asensi scored his second and Barca's third on 54 minutes when he picked up on a slack clearance deep in his half, beat three players unchallenged and cut through Real's left-hand side like a hot knife through butter, before finishing with a great left-foot strike. In the 65th minute, the Madrid players seemed to have collectively failed to grasp the concept of marking. Juan Carlos had the freedom of the Bernabéu, with a deep run from the halfway line to the 18-yard box, and deftly chipped Mariano García Remón to make it 4-0. The final goal deservedly fell to Sotil, who headed home brilliantly in the 69th minute after a perfectly weighted cross from a Cruyff free kick.

On the whistle, Cruyff sportingly found Netzer, shook hands and nonchalantly ran off the park as if he were out for an early evening jog. As well as being a brilliantly executed result for Barcelona, two fingers up to the federal government, and a display of some of the finest football seen in Spain in decades, the game had something even more interesting. An old-fashioned piece of football espionage. Tactically, you could see Michels had worked on something, but what? Asensi, Sotil and Marcial pulled and dragged and stretched, allowing Cruyff, playing slightly deeper, to thrive.

The victory was in fact down to a tactical move when Michels, acting on a tip-off, heard Real Madrid planned to adopt zonal marking to eliminate Cruyff's threat. At the time, a friend of Michels, Theo de Groot, whom he had once played with at Ajax, was living in Madrid. Theo, the father of sports journalist Jaap de Groot, lived beside Real centre-half Gregorio Benito, who often visited Michels. Cruyff laughed at the absurdity, before saying, 'He clearly didn't know anything about the relationship between de Groot and Michels because, before the match against Barcelona, he revealed Real's entire game plan. The core strategy was that I wouldn't be man-marked but marked zonally.'

Michels played him deeper and the confusion created holes everywhere which Cruyff and his team-mates were able to capitalise on. He may have been playing in Spain from October the previous year, but this result announced Barcelona were back. This was serious. Cruyff had barely arrived in Barcelona but already won over the Catalans by not only fighting to make sure his boy's name remained Jordi, the patron saint of Catalonia, but by deconstructing their rivals. He was already a hero.

Cruyff would immerse himself in the Catalan way and tradition. With regards to his political and social influence, in a *Guardian* obituary from 2016, Sid Lowe was most eloquent: 'Cruyff gave Barcelona a new identity and a new, sporting discourse that complemented and deepened the socio-political situation he came to understand and embrace so well; came to embody, in fact.'

Chapter 7

Reflection, the Early Years, and Jany van der Veen

CRUYFF WAS 31 and had become a global superstar. He was famous. However, growing up as he did, in a housing project, and losing his father aged 12, poverty would have seldom been far from his life. His father's best friend, 'Uncle Henke', who worked at Ajax, helped get his mother a job cleaning the house of the then manager Vic Buckingham and the other English coaches. Later, at Ajax, she would be employed to clean the offices and changing rooms; anything to put money on the table. Cruyff's background and where he grew up shaped the rest of his life. No matter the fame and success, everything would always come back to his childhood.

So, when he became a player and especially a coach, if he saw players behaving selfishly and not showing respect, he would think of the dressing rooms at Ajax his mother had to clean. Then of the dirty football kit – until Ajax became more professionally run – she would need to hand wash every day. Cruyff always had that in him. When everyone else was on holiday, and money was scarce, he would head to the stadium and end up playing baseball just to have people to hang out with.

The young Cruyff's athleticism – in the broader sense his reaction time, reflexes, his quick thinking – was allowed to flow and flourish naturally through the summers at Ajax. He attributes being able to understand and assimilate the concept and tactical approach of Total Football through playing baseball. For Johan, the club was like a community centre. Ajax had kids' baseball teams and he would show up at the stadium to see what was happening. At a loose end, he started to love baseball and found he was a competent catcher but was better at reading the game than playing. Unsurprisingly, and for mere mortals, quite annoyingly, he became proficient and found himself on the Dutch national team until he was 15.

Cruyff explained that playing baseball helped him understand and work out how to eventually read and analyse football: 'Baseball allowed me to focus on a lot of details that would later be very useful to me in football.' He learned the discipline and spatial awareness required to think ahead of the next play. 'You had to know where you were going to throw the ball before you received it, which meant that you had to have an idea of all the space around you and where each player was before you made your throw … It also taught me about tactical insight – making the right decision and performing it in a technically good way. It was only later that I pulled this together to create my vision of how the game of football should be played.'

Before Buckingham, another Englishman had an even greater impact on Ajax. Jack Reynolds was a visionary coach who not only managed but oversaw the running of the whole club, over three spells between 1915 and 1947. His approach, 4-3-3 with two wingers, interchanging passing and movement and with each side at the club playing the same way, set in place a template which would become the foundation for Ajax's Total Football. When he was arrested by the Germans in 1940 because he was British, the team's performance suffered.

Vic Buckingham was brought to Ajax for his first spell in 1960 and over two years won the Dutch title and the cup by playing a short passing game, focussing on possession of the ball and movement off it. His side scored lots of goals. Buckingham was a Spurs player before becoming a coach. He played at a time when Spurs themselves were undergoing a football revolution under Arthur Rowe, a coach who introduced a different, more fluid push-and-run style of play. Buckingham was a disciple of the short passing game and found success applying that style at amateur level before starting a coaching career which took him to West Bromwich Albion, Ajax, Sheffield Wednesday, Ajax again, Fulham, Barcelona, Sevilla and Olympiacos.

In his first spell at Ajax, he oversaw the development of the 12-year-old Cruyff and in his brief second spell in 1964, he gave the 17-year-old his debut. Ajax were in serious decline in this period and only narrowly avoided relegation. Buckingham reluctantly left when the Fulham job came up, so Rinus Michels came in and led the second rebirth.

Imagine for a second what it must be like to see a ten-year-old Cruyff, Pelé or Maradona? To witness them playing with their peer group, how commanding would they look? Would they stand out? Could you tell immediately they were going to become a star or would experience tell you that you'd seen it before? Let's keep calm and wait until the player has grown. You'd be aware there were pitfalls; potential injuries, bad luck, getting in with the wrong crowd, or would their ability be clear and so obvious? In *Brilliant Orange: The Neurotic Genius of Dutch Football*, David Winner interviewed Buckingham, 'He [Cruyff] was one who immediately struck a chord with me. As if he was my son. He was on his own and he showed us how to play. He was so mature. He was such a skinny little kid but he had such immense stamina. He could run all over the field. And he could do everything: set movements up, fly down the wing, run into the penalty area, head the ball in. Left foot, right foot, anything – and such speed. God's gift to mankind in the football sense. That was Johan. And such a nice kid as well.'

When Cruyff broke through and signed his first professional contract with Ajax, one of the first things he did was buy his mum a washing machine. At this time, players still took their dirty kit home. He also told her that she wouldn't be working at the club any longer. 'I signed the contract in the presence of my mother and when we left the office, I immediately told her that she'd cleaned the changing rooms for the last time the day before. I didn't want her to go to work to clean the room I'd just dirtied.'

It is remarkable to consider that when Cruyff made his first-team debut, in 1964, Ajax were still a semi-professional club. In 1965 he was offered his first full-time contract. Apart from Cruyff and Piet Keizer, the rest of the squad were still part-time, working during the day and only able to train in the evenings. Also, unbelievably, for a professional footballer,

Cruyff continued to play football with friends on the concrete streets of Betondorp, making himself prone to serious injury.

Keizer was a skilful and cultured left-winger from the Ajax Golden Age. He was also argumentative and headstrong. Like Cruyff, he was a club icon, playing 490 times, winning domestic and European titles, and appearing for the national side 34 times. After falling out with his boss, he also retired aged 31. Sadly, like Cruyff, Keizer also died of lung cancer.

With time on his hands, and now retired, out of choice and not injury, Cruyff would have been remembering the role models in his life, especially Jany van der Veen, who mentored and nurtured him at Ajax from the age of ten. It was Jany who spotted him in the street bossing older players and taking the ball around them. Van der Veen was the original one-club man. He served Ajax faithfully from 1939, joining as a player when the Second World War began. The war's impact upon mankind was devastating and of course, football is only a sport, but like most sides, Ajax felt the full force of the war. Jany was a crucial part of the side while the country recovered from the war and helped win the league and the KNVB Cup in 1947. He was ever-present and drove the club on. But one year later he retired after a bad injury. This was just after the Dutch famine, the Hongerwinter, in 1944–45, when German-occupied Netherlands blockaded shipments of food and fuel and brought the country to its knees. It was post-war Netherlands, people were traumatised from the horror of the conflict, and sports injuries from playing football were down the pecking order.

Jany also helped Rinus Michels when he retired from playing and became a coach. The men teamed up and would eventually play a crucial part in redefining the beautiful game. Jany was obsessed with football and scouting. Even after retiring from playing he was often found watching and nurturing talent around the club. At Ajax he proved to have an incredible eye for talent-spotting. As well as Cruyff he found Barry Hulshoff and Wim Suurbier. When Cruyff was named coach at Ajax in 1985, he made Jany van der Veen a scout and he found players like John Bosman, Aaron Winter and Edgar Davids.

In 1957, Van der Veen discovered and nurtured Cruyff. Ajax placed an importance on the growth and development of their youngsters as both footballers and people. Cruyff is always first to acknowledge the coach who took him under his wing.

Jany van der Veen quietly brought Cruyff into the club. He didn't offer him a trial; he had witnessed how good a player he was while watching him play on the street. He was welcomed in and allowed to develop and play. Jany worked with him on his football technique but instilled discipline. He knew Cruyff had the skill, but what he required was some guidance. He also taught him about life. Cruyff appreciated it, 'When I was at the Ajax youth team at the age of 12, Jany van der Veen trained me not only in football but also in morals and values. He was the first person at Ajax who taught me always to choose a particular course and follow it. He was the perfect example of how the Ajax life was one that compensated for the education that I wouldn't be getting at school.'

Cleaning your kit, and polishing and looking after your boots was important to him. It was something he would later instil as a coach to players in the youth sides coming through. It was important to understand the social aspect, learning life lessons, making people realise that these horrible jobs would teach them a bit of humility and to treat others better.

When Buckingham left and was replaced by Michels in 1965, the setup had become less professional. But within six years, Ajax would be conquering Europe and be the best club side in the world. In Cruyff's autobiography, he explains, 'Then, in 1971, we won the European Cup for the first time, and won it the next two years as well. So, within six years Ajax had gone from being an average club to the best team in the world. And what was the secret? It was simple – it was a combination of talent, technique and discipline, which were all things that we had been working on at Ajax, even before Rinus Michels had arrived.'

Chapter 8

Living in America, Road Trips with Wim

'It was wrong, a mistake, to quit playing at 31 with the unique talent I possessed. Starting from zero in America, many miles away from my past, was one of the best decisions I made. There, I learned how to develop my uncontrolled ambitions, to think as a coach and about sponsorship. America really was a blank slate. Everyone who'd been laughing at my misfortunes was far away in Europe, and I found my place completely in a new world.'

Johan Cruyff

CRUYFF, DUE to his financial situation, was forced to come out of retirement and accepted a lucrative offer to play in the North American Soccer League (NASL). While in the US, and feeling refreshed, the player realised he had to maximise his earning potential in the next three to four years. He would've hoped to have put his bad luck and ill-thought-through business decisions behind him. When playing in the US, we now know Cruyff was able to do something he rarely did due to the all-encompassing nature of his day job: he had time to think. The stress, pressure and constant hassle of playing at such an elite level, for Ajax and then Barcelona, had eased significantly. There was time to focus on his future while no doubt learning from his recent past. On the field and in training he continued to learn, watching and listening, but there was also a reality. His coaching days were rapidly approaching.

If Cruyff's final season at Feyenoord is often overlooked, his stay in the United States is practically airbrushed out of history. Cruyff's decision to play in the NASL was considered by many to be a lifestyle choice, not a football option. To Cruyff, it sounded perfect. Family first, and now, maybe for the first time, football was second.

With its usual haughtiness and snobbery, the European media slaughtered Cruyff for moving to America. The move was universally viewed as a gimmick; a publicity stunt or, more vulgar still, motivated by money. They may have had a point.

It was so unlike the Netherlands and Spain where everyone seemed to find fault in everything you did. He enjoyed the lifestyle too, where players were treated like adults, expected to act maturely and usually did, while away from the pitch.

The attraction for any player to conquer the USA was understandable. This nation was a vast sporting superpower, a country who knew how to hype up a show. They were capable of pumping up any event with razzmatazz and showbiz and knew how to put on a sporting show like no other, yet with soccer, despite excelling on the business side, at this point, they did not have a genuine connection with the game. Yet they would manage to beat many football nations to host the World Cup in 1994.

Since then, things have improved immeasurably, especially the women's game and the MLS but it takes time in sport, it's always about evolution, not revolution. Their kids always appear to be at soccer practice, so one day they might shock us all.

It was widely assumed that Cruyff was joining Pelé and Beckenbauer at New York Cosmos. He had discussions, but nothing detailed with the owners, the Ertegun brothers, from Atlantic Records who owned the club. Initially, Cruyff had signed a short-term pre-contract with New York Cosmos for $500,000. For this princely sum, he would play two exhibition games and simply give the club first option if he ever decided to play Stateside. Cruyff played one game but didn't like the AstroTurf, believing the game should be played on grass: 'The Giants Stadium was beautiful and impressive but after I'd played once on AstroTurf, I'd had enough. Artificial grass then was nothing like artificial grass today. It was kind of a carpet which meant you sometimes got enormous blisters on the soles of your feet.' For Cruyff, there was also a technical issue, the effect the surface had on the way the game was played. 'The ball also rebounded from it in a way that I wasn't used to. The Americans thought it was fantastic but as far as I was concerned it was out of the question to play football on a mat.' He was also discouraged by Cosmos star Franz Beckenbauer, who warned about both his and Pelé's contractual obligations to attend endless promotional activities. They were getting their money's worth.

Cruyff had made his mind up, he wanted to play for Rinus Michels at the Los Angeles Aztecs. They had both revolutionised the game in Europe and Cruyff firmly believed they would do it again, this time in the United States. The player had secured a

$500,000 salary, a huge amount, especially in football, in 1979. Those commentators and journalists poring over the move, misjudged Cruyff's intentions to make his presence felt in the United States. Cruyff loved America. He adored the positivity around the sport. He loved the culture, where achievement was respected and revered. A place where earning money wasn't frowned upon, the whole 'can-do' attitude suited him down to the ground. Professional sportspeople were respected and football clubs run in a far more business-like way.

The price to join up with the Dutch contingent at Aztecs instead of the Cosmos was $1m to get out of the contract. This was later reduced to $600,000, payable over three years. Cruyff continued with the voice of a football disciple and on arrival at LA he preached, 'Cosmos drew a lot of fans with Pelé. Even after he left they drew a lot of fans. So I thought my job should be on this coast.'

Cruyff finally joined up with Michels at the Aztecs in 1979. Michels was also clearly a huge fan of the game they called soccer, and the salary. Cruyff liked the way the Americans worked; contract negotiations were swift, remuneration generous and business done and dusted in hours, not weeks. Cruyff was amazed to be on a 12-hour flight to LA as soon as the contract was agreed and even more shocked to find he made his debut that evening, hours after landing. Many would be irritated at the speed of negotiation but Cruyff liked how the Americans worked and got the deal done. They got the business, the organisation and logistics right.

Within seven minutes of making his debut for the Aztecs, a jet-lagged and rather bemused Cruyff had scored twice and laid on one before leaving to a standing ovation. His playing record at the Aztecs was decent with 27 games, 14 goals and 14 assists, but the fans and club owner loved his attitude. His reputation was enhanced. He genuinely bought into the idea of spreading the word of the beautiful game, gave talks and seminars, and was keen to leave some kind of legacy with the club. He was also voted the league's Most Valuable Player.

In keeping with the fast-moving world of the US sports business, the club was sold to Televista, a company made up of Mexican investors. They wanted to wipe the slate clean and build a side of Mexican players, and Cruyff, once they saw his salary, was moved on.

Most would be dismayed but Cruyff looked at it in his way, turned the disadvantage into an advantage, and moved from the West Coast sunshine to the East Coast snow. He was off to Washington Diplomats. A change in the coast, weather, and a million dollars came his way. The Diplomats also took on the debt owed to the Cosmos. The only downside was that the football wasn't great.

The Dips were managed by an English coach called Gordon Bradley. Bradley was no forward-thinking leader like Rinus Michels. He was more of a kick and rush, more Burnley and Bolton than Barcelona or Bayern. Cruyff was under no illusions and there was no way they would win anything, so he did his thing and tried to organise, gel and coach the team.

Playing deeper and trying to control the games in an attempt to lift the side, he wasn't scoring. He was too stubborn to let it slide and continually tried to shout for more movement. As he dictated play, the technical level of his team-mates hit home. He was exasperated; no one was moving into space. The Washington Dips were bottom of the NASL, Cruyff still hadn't scored but he assumed his job was to sit deep and organise the players around him into some semblance of a team.

When the fans started to turn on him, due to his lack of goals, Cruyff took it personally, decided to entertain them, scored ten times and had 20 assists. He turned around their fortunes, though they were eliminated in the play-offs by his old employers, LA Aztecs.

If the football wasn't as exceptional as it should've been, the lifestyle off the park was fantastic. Cruyff found himself ingratiated by the movers and shakers of Washington. On his first outing with the Dips management, to an expensive Italian restaurant full of Washington's elite, no one gave Cruyff a second look. Not until the waiters, chefs and cleaners approached for a photograph and autograph and started surrounding and chatting to him. He was holding court; happy to finally speak to football people who couldn't believe who they were chatting with. Suddenly, to those present, he was someone.

The Washington Diplomats' chairman was a Democrat, so Cruyff and his family were welcomed to the party. Cruyff couldn't believe it when his celebrity had reached the point where the wives of the Kennedys tried to help him find a house. His neighbour was former Secretary of State Robert McNamara.

Cruyff was given full access to the football club. He could see how everything was run, from grassroots to the first team. He was also watching how experienced commercial director Andy Dolich operated in the hard-nosed business world, making deals, negotiating contracts and dealing with tough decisions. Not only was he learning on the pitch, but he was also starting to get a full flavour of how to run things behind the scenes.

As part of his contract, when they were at away games, Cruyff coached disabled children. He was hesitant at first, maybe nervous, but eventually realised he gained more as a person from the kids than he could ever give back. This sowed the seeds for the idea which would become the Johan Cruyff Foundation. It would eventually be set up in 1997 to provide opportunities for disabled kids to play sport. This would later grow to include underprivileged kids and poorer areas with Cruyff Courts. Cruyff knew the best way to learn and improve as a kid was to play constantly. The kids had stopped playing in the streets and the idea of safer courts in communities helped get them playing again.

The standard of player and Bradley's system could, for most, be tolerated but not for Cruyff's sensibilities. Where was the fluidity? The movement, the interchanging of positions. Playing deeper and instructing and continually haranguing players, they could only take so much of his criticism and started to go to the press, complaining Cruyff was a big-headed control freak, who was breaking and destroying their confidence.

It wasn't solely the players as Cruyff was laying into the board, requesting upgrades to first-class travel and less time on training, especially in the blistering Washington summers, and a more flexible itinerary while on the road. He approached the Diplomats' management to set up a second and third team so younger players could get used to playing, work on technique and gain experience. If they played well they would be promoted to the first team squad, be on to the bench, be around the changing rooms and gain experience of being involved on a match day.

While playing for the Diplomats, Cruyff and his former Dutch team-mate and friend Wim Jansen would make the most of boring journeys to away games by hiring a car and going on road trips. They would go off for a few hours visiting and exploring random towns. Cruyff and Jansen had come through together; Cruyff was a few months older and they were close. On one occasion when they played an away game in New York, they wanted to visit the World Trade Center but when there was a massive queue, Cruyff decided to hire two blazers to make them look like a couple of businessmen, or security guards, and made for the second tower, which didn't have tourists. They took the elevator to the top floor and saw the best view of New York.

When Bradley would give a long-winded team talk, Cruyff would stand up, wipe the blackboard clean and tell those present how they would play instead. It was rude, unheard of and undermined the coach but the players did what he suggested and started to win.

All of Cruyff's actions indicated that he was there for a reason. He bought in to raising the standard and changing the system. He liked the NASL, and the opportunity had given him a blank canvas. He genuinely wanted to and believed he could build something there. He loved the way they treated soccer as an entertainment entity and that the fans were pivotal in that relationship. He liked their ideas, experimenting with the game, especially the 35-yard shootout instead of penalties.

Cruyff's short time at the Dips might best be summed up by a quote from club president Steve Danzansky, 'He was like a great musician – with perfect pitch – who was forced to play in an orchestra where everybody around him was playing off-key. It drove him completely nuts.'

When Cruyff considered the move, the aim was to help bring football in America on, to revolutionise and recalibrate it. It could be argued that doing so may have been a great idea, but when he was aged just 31 was too early in the development of the game there. Football people did not accept America would or could conquer the game those Stateside called soccer. The trouble was that most of the big stars who moved there were past their best. Cruyff was younger than both Pelé and Beckenbauer, and still able to play at the top level.

Cruyff was too early for America. They weren't ready for him in 1979. He was about continual improvement, education and development. But years later, on reflection, he remained upbeat and positive about what he tried to do in the States, 'I'm still a bit proud to have been one of those people, along with Pelé, Franz Beckenbauer, Johan Neeskens and all the rest, who pioneered the rise of football in that still-developing continent. When I see how football is improving there, I know it's just a matter of time before an American team wins the World Cup. As a football lover, I'd think that would be great.'

Let's briefly jump forward to 1994 and CONCACAF. The American contingent at FIFA have the power and contacts and overflowing gift bags and have somehow been able to award that summer's FIFA World Cup to the USA. The 1994 tournament was universally regarded as one of the most woeful competitions yet. There was something not right, something in the spirit of it, or the soul of the game. It felt fake. The weather was too hot, matches were scheduled for the wrong time of the day and the grass on the pitches was too long.

The finals started with Diana Ross missing a penalty from six yards out with a massive ball, and the playing of the tournament's official song, a woeful number sung by Daryl Hall called 'Gloryland'. It never recovered from that low. The world was furious at a country that, at least then, had no professional league, hosting the World Cup. The USA was perceived to know nothing about football and called it soccer instead. It was the wrong fit. The truth is that America isn't a football nation. Brazil, Argentina, Germany, Italy, Spain, Netherlands, England and Scotland are established football nations. The US and its states are too truncated and varied, so they are united by their sports; American football, basketball, baseball and NASCAR. Some of the colder states even prefer ice hockey before soccer.

When you consider what Cruyff packed in to his two years in the NASL you could argue it was one of the most formative times of his career. He learned skills which would influence the rest of his life such as the commercial side, his worth as a player, how to negotiate for a share of ticket sales in home gates, coaching kids, tactics, people skills, and how a club is run from top to bottom. He also understood how to be more effective and concise when dealing with TV reporters and the media. When he quit coaching in 1996, he would be able to naturally turn his hand to analysing football on TV and would also have a spiky, controversial football column.

Cruyff played the 1980 season for the Diplomats, despite the club facing financial ruin. He returned to Ajax in November 1980 as a technical adviser to Leo Beenhakker. The side were eighth in the league when he joined and finished second. He also played three games in friendlies for FC Dordrecht. While back in Europe for the off-season and intending to return to the Dips, Cruyff was injured when appearing as a guest for AC Milan in a tournament, forcing him to miss the start of the Diplomats' 1981 season. It was then that he decided to leave.

I remember the palpable excitement around the news Cruyff was about to sign for Leicester City in February 1981. The deal appeared to be on. After a promising start in the league, Leicester were bottom and needed something. Manager Jock Wallace knew Cruyff and worked out his high wages would be a price worth paying if he kept Leicester in the First Division.

However, negotiations were taking an age and after three weeks, the deal fell through. Imagine Johan Cruyff on *Match of the Day*? The player was offered £4,000 a week, an eye-watering amount of money in 1980/81. According to official figures released by the PFA, there were only eight players in England earning a basic salary of £50,000 per year back then. This would be around £962 a week for top players, who would also have bonuses. The average player wage was around £600 per week.

Cruyff moved to Valencia, playing for Levante in March 1981, in an attempt to get them promoted to LaLiga. A combination of injuries and fall-outs with the club saw him play only ten games, scoring twice.

Chapter 9

Season 1983/84:
Matchdays 8–13

SOME OF Cruyff's play in his year-long adventure in Rotterdam beggars belief. His burst of pace allowed him to go around anyone who dared to tackle him. As soon as they committed, Cruyff was half a second ahead and would accelerate beyond them. Passing with both feet sounds like something professional footballers should be able to do but often they can't or if they can, they don't have the confidence to do it.

Even at this point in his career, aged 36, watching Cruyff play is such a privilege and joy. At first, it's not obvious why he is so special. Then you slowly realise, as you watch more, that it's his positioning, and it seems like he can pass the ball using every part of his foot. And then you have his 'sprint within the sprint', which allows him to rapidly accelerate. Yes, and he could read the game like a mathematician, knew how to make use of space; when he passed to Gullit or Hoekstra, the third man had to be running into a free area – it looked choreographed and seemed to flow so naturally.

The game was an overlapping whirling dervish of one-touch dazzle, played at a ferocious pace and tempo. As he got older, coaches correctly advised him to run less in training, telling him he was fit enough. He only needed to keep the engine ticking over.

Cruyff had proven throughout his career that he thought differently from other players and coaches when it came to effort and work rate. He had an unusual approach. Cruyff's mantra on running, fitness, exertion and effective use of energy was continually repeated, 'Every trainer talks about movement, about running a lot and putting a shift in. I say don't run as much. Football is a game you play with your brains. You have to be in the right place at the right moment, not too early, not too late.'

Cruyff was still shouting, coaching and conducting. Focus was still on the first touch, keeping possession, vision, seeking out the correct pass, playing with intelligence and style. It meant playing wide, stretching the game, passing and interplay.

He made the ball do most of the work. Some of his skills, like the trivela, involved putting spin and curve on the ball when shooting. Passing or crossing with the outside of the foot was used more readily. One of his biographers, Nico Scheepmaker, once described him as four-footed. As ridiculously comedic as this sounds, when you watch him spray passes with the outside of his left and right foot, you can understand what Scheepmaker meant. Cruyff reminded us, even in the twilight of his career, why we called it the beautiful game, one which should and often did bring boundless joy to many.

On matchday eight, Feyenoord played for the first time since their humiliating defeat at the hands of Ajax. They hosted sixth-placed Go Ahead Eagles, from Deventer. The opposition and the previous result could've been a factor in a low crowd of 21,609.

Cruyff's old Netherlands team-mate Jan Jongbloed was in goal for Go Ahead Eagles. When I say old, I do mean old; he was 43, and still making wonderful saves and keeping his team in the game. When Vermeulen played up the left flank to Cruyff, he crossed a perfect ball to Houtman who powerfully headed it towards the right-hand post. Jongbloed's save was reminiscent of Gordon Banks's 1970 World Cup save from Pelé's header.

By now, as the season started to settle – perhaps it's the maxim among football players and coaches that it takes at least eight games to find your match fitness and touch – Cruyff's influence was obvious, actively encouraging and bringing out the best in those around him. Gullit scored twice and would end the season having scored 15. Houtman would net 21 goals. Hoekstra would score 19. So the goals were shared out, which was how Cruyff liked it, with the midfield breaking through and attacking and scoring. Ajax striker Marco van Basten was the Eredivisie's top scorer that season with 28 goals.

The first goal against Go Ahead Eagles came after poor defending. Cruyff played a speculative left-footed pass through the central position, and when it was cleared, Gullit capitalised and nonchalantly took it round the keeper.

In the second half again, Jongbloed came to the rescue, stopping bravely at Gullit's feet. The second goal came after some fine work from Vermeulen, who started the move in his own half, playing a one-two with Cruyff, before racing into the box. He managed to cut back with a low cross, which was headed home by Gullit on 74 minutes. Cruyff had a great chance late on when he received the ball in the centre from Gullit and took it around four players with his trademark burst of pace, dipped his shoulder, made to hit it, then banged a great left-footed shot off the post. The game ended 2-0.

With a break for the Dutch Cup, matchday nine would see Feyenoord head to AZ Alkmaar. If they had the time they could've popped into the Beatles Museum – John Lennon's first guitar was made in Alkmaar. Better still, they may have fancied a visit to the famous cheese market.

André Hoekstra scored the only goal, in the 76th minute. Alkmaar keeper Eddie Treytel made several wonderful saves. The Feyenoord goal came from a huge kick out from their goalkeeper, Joop Hiele. The ball bounced high and Houtman reached it first, knocking it into the path of Hoekstra who scored from a tight angle. Simple direct football and, a well-taken goal. Best of all, another two points on the board.

The sun shone brightly on Feyenoord's De Kuip for the visit of third-placed PSV Eindhoven on matchday ten. A bumper crowd of 33,076, showed up to see a 1-1 draw with Jan Reker's PSV. Feyenoord took the lead in the 57th minute after a whipped free kick came into the box and Houtman headed down to Andrey Zhelyaskov, but in the 71st minute, Jurrie Koolhof headed in a deserved equaliser. The goal came from a perfectly weighted cross from full-back Berry van Aerle. Forget starring for PSV and playing for the Dutch national side 35 times, with a name like Berry van Aerle he should have been starring on the Motown record label. PSV played well and looked a great side, tight and quick with loads of creativity and movement, especially through the middle. Then again, they had a certain whippersnapper called Arie Haan, aged 35, playing there.

Next for Feyenoord was a trip to Maastricht to take on Sportvereniging Roda Juliana Combinatie Kerkrade, or thankfully for sub-editors, Roda JC. A 16,500 crowd witnessed a comprehensive 4-0 victory for the visitors on a bright, sunny, autumn day. Gullit almost scored from a Hoekstra cross early on but the deadlock was broken in the 34th minute when a speculative ball from Cruyff was met by Gullit, who managed to head it on to Zhelyaskov to loop his header high over the advancing Roda keeper Jos Smits for his sixth goal of the season. Six minutes later, some neat work from Cruyff took him past three Roda players, before playing in Gullit, who cut back for Zhelyaskov to score his second.

Hoekstra scored twice in the second half, taking his tally for the season to six. His first came after driving down the right before finishing with a powerful shot. The second came from a made-to-measure cross from Gullit, wide on the right, and Hoekstra's headed finish was superb. With two goals each for two midfielders, a 4-0 scoreline and the points on the board it was job done for Feyenoord.

A familiar name for Birmingham, Aberdeen and Dunfermline fans – one Jimmy Calderwood – played for Roda. Jimmy looked whiter than normal.

Excelsior's visit on matchday 12 to take on Feyenoord pulled a crowd of 21,161. Those present witnessed Cruyff score twice in one of his better games that season. His first goal came in the 17th minute after the Excelsior keeper Jan Stroomberg mis-hit a goal kick (or perhaps we can be charitable and blame it on the strong wind). Cruyff showed that he still had great speed of thought, reacting quickest to take the ball around Stroomberg and finishing with his left foot. His second goal and his fourth of the season came in the 42nd minute and was vintage Cruyff. He won the ball from a laid-back opponent inside the opposition half in a central position, and sprinted off, eventually taking it around the goalkeeper, finishing it off like his first goal with a whipped left-foot shot. Hoekstra scored the third goal, his seventh of the season, in the 68th minute before turning provider with a great run, cutting it back for Gullit to tap in for the fourth on 87.

Matchday 13 saw a comprehensive 4-1 defeat in a local derby at Sparta Rotterdam as 20,000 welcomed Feyenoord. The visitors had to remain patient but were finally rewarded in the 70th minute when Pierre Vermeulen scored with a header at the back post. The second, six minutes later, was also header from a cross from the right and scored at the back post by Hoekstra. Houtman despatched a penalty to make it 3-0 before Hoekstra's second made it four on 89 minutes. Ronald Lengkeek scored an injury-time consolation for Sparta.

Sparta had future Netherlands coach Danny Blind in defence that day, and a certain Louis van Gaal in midfield. Later in life, Cruyff and van Gaal fell out quite spectacularly and didn't mind people knowing about it. During the match Gullit was taken out by Sparta keeper Bas van Noortwijk with a kick to the solar plexus. No card was given, indeed no free kick was awarded, and there was no sympathy for the Feyenoord man. Football from this era was a different game.

Chapter 10

The Movie and Number 14

WHEN AJAX won the Intercontinental Cup in 1972 to be recognised as the best club side in the world, Cruyff had become an international star and was one of the planet's most recognised players. He had something else though. It wasn't just his football ability, he had that star quality; he was different and played with confidence and freedom. He looked great on the park, stylish off it, and of course, was not short of an opinion.

Cruyff was seriously famous in the late 1960s and 1970s at a time when football stars were roped into the most idiotic business decisions, like making terrible records. In 1969, Cruyff, sensationally pop pickers, joined the likes of The Who, and Jimi Hendrix on Polydor records, when he recorded a charity single called, 'Oei Oei Oei (Dat Was Me Weer Een Loei)'. Cruyff sings like an inebriated Benny Hill in a drunken knees-up pub song. It's still better than Hoddle and Waddle's 'Diamond Lights'. Cruyff reached number 21 in the Dutch charts.

Looking back, it feels like a strange and awkward time for the more famous players. There they were, famous and rich, but living in an era when there seemed a generation gap between them and the older players and managers. George Best opened hip and groovy shops, something they could fall back on once their career was over. Cruyff opened a boutique shoe shop called Shoetique, in December 1969, in Kinkerstraat, Amsterdam.

Celebrities in the 1970s were requested to do some incredibly stupid things. Cruyff, for instance, advertised a painting company. That must have been an interesting meeting. 'Well look, he's often compared to an artist, so why don't we have him in to advertise our painter and decorator business?' Easy money, I suppose, for a few hours' work. 'Here Johan, put on these overalls and grab that brush.' It shows how much the game has moved on financially. Players used to advertise for local car companies, hotels or breweries. On one occasion Cruyff was invited to open the latest super-chic hotel by kicking a ball through the window of the door and smashing glass everywhere. Thousands showed up to see him, too (Health and Safety Dave would have had a field day). Thankfully, he was only a successful footballer and not a nuclear physicist who had invented a portable anti-aircraft rocket launcher. The player hit supersonic stardom in the 1970s to the extent that a movie was made about him.

In 1972, director Maarten de Vos made a movie about Johan Cruyff. He filmed him playing to a weird, early Dutch porn jazz kind of soundtrack. The movie is called *Nummer 14 Johan Cruiyff*. It follows him arriving for training and back at home; the usual footballer's life scenes. The film was produced by his father-in-law and agent, Cor Coster, and recorded Cruyff's every move.

I'm not sure if *The Sweeney* ever made it to Dutch TV but that's what this movie looks like. It opens with cool cars and players arriving at training. Then we see the older coach, Stefan Kovács, like someone out of *Dad's Army*, smiling and happy as he arrives for training on his bike. We cut to the Intercontinental Cup (a FIFA competition where the European Cup winners took on the winners of the Copa Libertadores – the club equivalent of the top South American sides) as Ajax face Independiente, from Argentina.

Cool jazz flutes continue to play over Cruyff running up and down steep slopes, stretching, then driving home in his super-cool car to his family. It's a typical 1970s football player in the kitchen scene with the cute child being cheeky as dad eats breakfast and loving wife looks on. While driving, we witness Johan putting some state-of-the-art futuristic cassette into the car's space-age console.

The film looks every bit like 1972 and captured the player, the epitome of 1970s fashion, long hair, sitting perfectly, short-sleeved shirt, superbly. We cut to him playing a game. It's in slow motion, his effortless style and wonderful skill making him ideal for the role. He looks so relaxed. His long legs are always twisting and turning in a stunningly balletic scene.

The narrative in this movie, and it's a subtle one – well as subtle as the idea of a movie being co-produced by your agent and father-in-law can be – is that Cruyff had outgrown Ajax. You sense throughout that Johan wouldn't be in Amsterdam for much longer. There was already a feeling of foreboding that he was off. He had now become too cool and famous for the Dutch mentality. He had outgrown Ajax. It was clear he was heading for Madrid or Barcelona, or somewhere big enough for the global superstar. The movie captured the moment his career kicked into overdrive.

Cruyff's life had changed. It happens to everyone who hits his level of fame. It seems to get bigger and crazier. He had won the European Cup and had been named European Footballer of the Year in 1971 but there was a clear build up in his profile. At Ajax, the club seems serene and calm and despite their success, it's all very cosy, compact and basic. In training, the players all show up with different training gear on. For context, let's remember that this is still 1972 so if Cruyff were The Beatles, at Ajax, he was starting to whip it up in the UK but would've just played *Val Parnell's Sunday Night at the London Palladium*, in October 1963, watched by 15 million viewers.

By the time Cruyff upped his profile with a combination of his expensive transfer to Barcelona in 1973, and his impact with both Total Football and the Cruyff Turn at the 1974 World Cup in West Germany, his fame had hit The Beatles arriving in New York and playing the *Ed Sullivan Show* on 9 February 1964. After that, everything changed globally. His level of fame went into superstar mode. Suddenly the world knew his name.

We see Cruyff training again, then it's an Eredivisie game, and as he leaves, he's signing autographs for adoring fans as sports, news and film crews interview him. They follow him with microphones stuck in his face. It's claustrophobic. He's too big for Ajax. Then we have the subtle reminders not to get too big-headed. Fans look lovingly and nervously at their hero, hand him a scrap of paper and a pen and Johan signs. The player looked like a rock 'n' roll star at times. He had the look of a punk rocker – he was CBGB (Country, BlueGrass and Blues) thin, the guitarist in a new wave underground band who everyone thought was going to make it big but became an insurance man. Amid the clamour and shouting, something makes him stop for a second. He smiles, remembering he was one of them, no, he *is* one of them, he got lucky. He is an Amsterdammer, he was that poor kid waiting to see his heroes. He signs another few autographs.

The movie cuts to more extraordinary slow-motion moves of the return leg of the Intercontinental Cup at the Olympic Stadium, against Independiente, on 28 September 1972. The first leg in La Doble Visera ended in a 1-1 draw. We watch the brutality and confusion as Argentine players try to tackle and kick Cruyff, who is leaping over and around assaults. He avoids and tilts and steps over and meanders around them.

In one scene, Cruyff is marked tightly by an opponent as he runs quickly with the ball. This move was reminiscent of one of Cruyff's most famous goals. It has entered folklore for several reasons. Firstly, because it was so outrageous – secondly because no film of it exists anywhere. Any reports only exist anecdotally in oral form.

Ajax were playing in a friendly against an amateur side, when Cruyff broke through on goal and, with only the goalkeeper to beat, turned around and began running away from him with the ball. The goalkeeper continued to chase him, reaching the halfway line before starting to sense something wasn't quite right. Cruyff no longer had the ball. When the keeper turned around, Cruyff had scored without breaking his stride by quickly back-heeling it into the net. He had kept on running while pretending he had the ball.

In this particular move, as the Independiente player tracks him with his eyes locked in on his target, the ball is no longer there and hasn't been for a while. Cruyff has magically made it disappear while running at speed, and keeping his stride, expertly back-heeling it to his team-mate while his opponent still chased him. It's as clever as his famous turn. If you listen closely enough you can hear the sound of the ball laughing.

Then we move to a tense scene in the Independiente game. Cruyff is debating and discussing the game with his coach, Kovács, on the touchline. It looks like he's telling his boss how to do his job during the game, which Ajax won 3-0.

Then the Cruyff family are filmed at a swish award ceremony and Johan is receiving his Ballon d'Or with his daughter and wife. We go to his devoted mum and are then taken to Betondorp, back to where he grew up, and those who knew him and his pals, saying how, even as a kid, he was amazing at football. The housing project doesn't look as bad as you'd imagine from the post-war bleakness often portrayed in other publications. It looks nice and clean, the gardens are well-tended, and the people there are friendly. Cruyff laughs a lot, nodding to say that yes, even as a kid he wouldn't pass the ball to those older than him, and would dribble around them repeatedly. The older guys are saying something cheeky about him and he's blushing. The neighbours are friendly, and know him well and reminisce. He leaves the kids with their grandmother and heads off, waving on his way.

Back at home, while discussing the European Cup Final victory against Inter Milan that same year, he puts a chunky-looking video cassette into the first Philips video model, the N1500. It looks so cool. Then as if by magic we are in real film footage of the game. I would've kept a video of that game too if I were Cruyff. It was one of his best games in an Ajax shirt. He was the man of the match, scored two goals and his side showcased their Total Football philosophy on the European stage. Then we cut to the European Cup being paraded through Amsterdam.

Nummer 14 Johan Cruiyff is of its time and delightful. The movie may have been named after Cruyff's shirt but, contrary to public opinion, it wasn't always his number, and again it came about by accident. For around the first six years of his career at Ajax, he played in the number nine shirt. Later at Barca, he also wore nine. In those days, the football authorities across Europe were incredibly officious and strict about players wearing the correct number corresponding to their position on the field. When Ajax were facing PSV, in October 1970, Cruyff's team-mate Gerry Muhren couldn't find his usual lucky number seven shirt and was a bit miffed. So Cruyff offered him his nine shirt and took a spare from the Ajax kit basket, which happened to be the 14. When Ajax won, Cruyff was adamant that he and Muhren keep the same shirt numbers for the following game. There was an element of mischief-making, too, as Cruyff loved to wind up the authorities. He knew that by flouting the rules he would annoy the beaks who check the team-sheets at the KNVB.

The number issue would also create problems for the international side. We know those who run football associations across the globe detest people like Cruyff, with their youthful rebellion. When manager Rinus Michels named a squad the players were given shirt numbers alphabetically. The Dutch FA demanded that Cruyff, who in alpha order was number one, must wear that shirt. He wouldn't do it. Michels allowed him to have number 14. There was also another characteristic display of defiance in 1974 when Cruyff, who had a lucrative contract with Puma, declined to play in the Dutch side's Adidas-manufactured strip. Most other players would've been dropped. Not Cruyff. It created a headache and required some alteration so a stripe was lost from his shirt.

Ajax eventually retired the famous number 14 shirt in 2007.

Chapter 11

Ajax and the European Cup Finals

1969

Ajax's run of European success from 1966 was a remarkable turnaround, the improvement in their performance levels showing that they were indeed heading somewhere. Their first European Cup Final saw them face AC Milan, in Madrid in 1969.

Ajax looked like they lacked experience, and a big-game cutting edge. That would come eventually, but at this point they were not ready. This final was too early for them in their development. Milan played them off the park and Ajax were no match for Nereo Rocco's men. AC Milan's side was full of experience. Pierino Prati would go into the history books when he scored the first European Cup Final hat-trick since Hungarian legend Ferenc Puskás in 1962. Angelo Sormani scored the Rossoneri's other goal in the 4-1 win.

There was one noteworthy event though; the crowd in Real Madrid's Santiago Bernabéu Stadium applauded Cruyff off the park after his display. AC Milan captain Gianni Rivera was also generous in his praise, 'We won 4-1 against a very young

Ajax side, young but good. Cruyff was at the beginning but already you knew what he would become. Despite the defeat, the Bernabéu applauded him, and they know a great footballer.'

Ajax were beaten but Cruyff saw it as a learning curve, something they had to deal with, recover from and move on. They were comprehensively given a football lesson and got off lightly at 4-1. This would prove to be quite the period for Dutch football. Austrian Ernst Happel had guided his Feyenoord side to their first final of the European Cup, narrowly beating Scottish champions and favourites, Celtic, in the 1970 final at Milan's San Siro stadium.

1971

On a bright summer evening in London, Ajax took on Greek champions Panathinaikos. The opening goal came after five minutes when Piet Keizer skipped down the left and bulleted in a low cross for 'Dick' van Dijk to head in at the front post. Dirk Wouter Johannes 'Dick' van Dijk (15 February 1946–8 July 1997) could not have been nicknamed anything else. He was a popular member of the squad, scoring 56 goals in 84 league appearances over three years. He was often a sub but always delivered when called upon.

After he stopped playing, Van Dijk lived in Nice, in Saint-Paul-de-Vence. He died suddenly of acute endocarditis, a bacterial infection on the heart, aged 51, but will always have a place in Ajax hearts, and club folklore.

Arie Haan scored the second in the 87th minute after some clever wide play by Cruyff, who played the perfect pass for Haan to fire home from close range.

1972

It was ironic, given where he would end his career, that one of Johan Cruyff's finest games would occur in the 1972 European Cup Final at De Kuip stadium. The home of Feyenoord and Cruyff's future club – some 12 years off – was electric. The crowd were mostly made up of fans of the Dutch side, who had made the short trip. The script felt as if it was already written for Cruyff. Here was one of the finest footballers the Netherlands had ever produced, who was attracting attention the world over, playing a European final against Inter Milan, in his home country. Cruyff's reputation had preceded him and he found he was tightly marked yet would go on to give one of his best displays in an Ajax shirt, if not his whole career.

This was an important evening for Ajax for several reasons. The club, as holders, were irritated at suggestions they had been lucky to win the trophy the previous season. Their victory was dismissed as a one-off and even their opponents in the final at Wembley the previous year were the unfancied Greeks, Panathinaikos. Ajax were determined to prove it was no fluke. A victory against a giant like Inter Milan would confirm their arrival as a potent force in European football. The final itself would also set up an intriguing subplot. This would be a meeting of two football philosophies. This was Total Football taking on catenaccio.

Ajax continued to work on their system, refining and tweaking what would become known as the Total Football template. This style of play was set in motion by Rinus Michels and now continued by Stefan Kovács. By 1972, Michels had waved goodbye to Amsterdam and headed for the sunshine of Barcelona. His work at Ajax was done, having turned an ailing and struggling club into European Cup winners. It was quite remarkable. His formula of technique and discipline was making him a wanted man. His replacement, the avuncular Kovács, was in charge and with Cruyff emerging as a major European star, they led Ajax to their second consecutive European Cup Final.

This style of play would not become known as Total Football until later, when it was popularised by the Netherlands at the 1974 World Cup and a journalist coined the phrase. Back in 1972, Ajax had started to add some power to the defensive side of the system, something which would be improved upon again for the tournament in West Germany two years later. By then knowledge of the system was starting to become more widespread due to more games being televised, especially matches like the European Cup Final.

Inter Milan played their classic Italian game with an approach that their reputation was built on; catenaccio. They soaked up pressure, closed down, defended patiently, then hit quickly on the counter attack. The Italians love this but many neutrals are prone to shout, 'What's Italian for parking the bus?' However, if catenaccio is played correctly, it doesn't necessarily have to be defensive. It should be used as security for anything breaching the defensive line.

Inter's world-renowned coach Helenio Herrera is most associated with the system but, like Total Football, it had more to do with an Austrian, Karl Rappan. While coaching at the Swiss club Servette in Geneva, Rappan grew irritated as his part-time side toiled against fitter, full-time teams. Rappan devised a system of play which allowed his side to rest, set up to absorb and then hit on the counter-attack.

Rappan refused to stick to the received wisdom of the favoured formation of the time, 2-3-5. He utilised two of his wing-backs as defenders, and the inside-forward and centre-half would play in a midfield three. The full-backs would play as two centre-backs and when they were under pressure, the spare man, 'the bolt', would slide along behind to cover. Catenaccio is translated as 'door bolt'.

He utilised the system when he became Switzerland manager in 1937 and received wonderful plaudits and acclaim when his side beat Germany. Catenaccio gained further fame and became more commonplace when it was adopted in post-war Italy.

Rather than give Rappan any credit, it eventually entered into folklore that the system was formed when the struggling Salernitana coach Gippo Viani walked early one morning along the shoreline and looking out to sea watched a bobbing trawler pull in its haul. It used the main net and behind it, they were using a reserve, a second net, to catch the fish the first net had missed. When he applied the same principles to his struggling defensive setup, the transformation was immediate and Salernitana eventually achieved promotion into Serie A.

Unfortunately, Viani would not be able to win games away from home against better quality opposition and was relegated but, again, let's not allow the cold, hard facts to spoil such a wonderful piece of romanticism. Defending should be about pragmatism though, not idealism.

Nereo Rocco had performed miracles as coach of struggling Triestina when he was appointed in 1947, using the system, and when he became boss of AC Milan he effectively employed it in 1961/62 when his side won Serie A and the following season's European Cup.

Herrera won the European Cup the following two years using the same system. So take your choice. Rappan, Viani or Rocco, or maybe all three, had used and evolved catenaccio. The system would, as Total Football had done, slightly evolve and be effectively used by Herrera.

The 1972 European Cup Final in Rotterdam served up the two best sides in Europe and highlighted two distinct football cultures.

Inter Milan had beaten Celtic in their semi-final. The game was level after the first leg, level again after 90 minutes of the second, and extra time couldn't separate the sides so the tie went to a penalty shootout. For the purists, a final between Ajax and Celtic with two clubs schooled on entertaining, attacking and goal-filled matches might have been a better spectacle. It would have been a curious cultural contest with both teams having an attacking philosophy and coaches who demanded goals.

This was an Inter side containing Giacinto Facchetti, one of the finest defenders Italian football had ever produced. He captained Italy to the European Championship in 1968. Inter's skipper Alessandro Mazzola was an experienced striker and international, and both players had won the European Cup with their club in 1963 and 1964. Mazzola scored twice in the 1964 final against Real Madrid.

This game is regarded as one of Cruyff's best but, as brilliant as his performance was, it would be wrong to highlight him in a system which relies so heavily on teamwork. Cruyff agreed, 'Of course, I had my own special qualities, but a team is formed by every player's different qualities – no player can do it on their own. Then, when every player is ready to give their all and use their special quality, then you get the maximum output and results.'

Herrera was skilled in devising how not to lose games; any opposition who beat them had to be astute and creative. For those watching the final in Rotterdam, this must have been a watershed moment. Perhaps it was not as exciting or high-scoring as Real Madrid and Eintracht Frankfurt at Hampden, in 1960, but those in the stadium or watching live on TV must've sensed something special was happening and the rule book was being re-written. This was the first high-profile match in the modern era and the way football was being played was unique.

Ajax's game was about pressing opponents and keeping possession. As they probed, Inter, as masters of defensive football, defended. There was more passing, fewer long balls and goalkeepers played it out more, starting moves from the back. Ajax pressed high in Inter's half and attacked. It was as simple as that. They played with rhythm, created chances and any time they were in the central position, they shot at goal.

These days we have become used to, especially in major finals, seeing sides set up and start slowly, but in this game, Ajax displayed high-pressing, attacking football. But we also had Inter, when the opportunity arose, trying to break up the park and counter attack. On several occasions, they came close to breaking through but were either stopped by some tough tackling or Ajax playing a high offside line. It shouldn't be ignored that, along with the plaudits for attacking, Ajax were still cute defensively, especially pushing out quickly to catch Inter offside.

The central part of their game was always to press or possess and Ajax were constantly attacking Inter in the first half. They worked harder to win the ball back. The pressing wasn't as intensive or as frenzied as the approach Netherlands boss Rinus Michels took against Sweden in the group stage of the 1974 World Cup, when some of their pressing in that game looked like a gang committing an assault. Ajax weren't pressing as chaotically or aggressively yet but there was a huge element of that.

Total Football needs controlled aggression to win the ball back, followed by a burst of creativity. Cruyff and Neeskens played with so much energy and Ajax seemed to possess more freedom, attacking without fear. They were also quick to stifle any counter attacks from Inter and expertly handled their star striker Roberto Boninsegna. Johan Neeskens did a superb marking job on Mazzola. Inter had a great and experienced side but couldn't seem to cope with the pace, energy and probing of Ajax.

It wasn't all grandstanding and showing off from Ajax. When they needed to defend, they did so robustly. In the 11th minute, Facchetti and Guibertoni, two Inter defenders, broke. Facchetti lobbed the ball through the left flank on to a brilliant run from Guibertoni, who reached it and skilfully turned inside, only to be sliced down by the Ajax rearguard.

The referee allowed play to continue, no free kick was awarded or bookings handed out to anyone. To add insult to injury, Ajax broke up the park and came close to scoring. Guibertoni had to be replaced after 12 minutes.

It was one of the elements often airbrushed out of the 'beautiful game' and Total Football narrative but Ajax, especially with their defence and defensive midfielders, knew how to mix it and go in hard. In fact, they were expected to. The main aim of most opponents was to stop Cruyff. One of the qualities seldom mentioned when describing his many great attributes was his courage. In keeping with this style of player and particularly during this era, they were continually booted and kicked but got up and got on with it. The referees seemed unfamiliar with career-ending tackles.

Throughout the final, Inter's defence performed well, at times forcing Cruyff to go hunting elsewhere. Gabriele Oriali was adept at full-back and in midfield and renowned for his tough tackling, stamina and ball-winning abilities. He played well, trying to contain Cruyff, but was pulled inside-out by the Dutchman. Cruyff started to shine when he broke ranks, coming deep to take the ball and driving on. His bursts of pace and work rate were noticeable and he gave his opponents a torrid time.

The two goals weren't Cruyff's best but they were two of his most significant. Both came in the second half. The first was fortuitous; a deep, speculative cross from Sjaak Swaart was misjudged by goalkeeper Ivano Bordon and the Inter defence, and it fell to Cruyff who couldn't have hoped for an easier tap-in.

The second came from a corner in the 78th minute. The header was exquisite, great technically and perfectly executed as Cruyff rose high to score. However, Cruyff's subtle movement before the ball reached him made the goal. Cruyff casually wandered from his marker for a few yards. When the ball was crossed, it bought him some crucial time and space and the Inter defenders couldn't get to him. He had sealed the second consecutive European Cup win and the Ajax fans present at De Kuip were ecstatic.

It is noticeable that Ajax had ten Dutch players and one German in their team while Inter fielded ten Italians and one Brazilian, in stark contrast to today's game. Football has gone global now but both clubs reached extraordinarily great heights mostly with homegrown players.

1973

The third European Cup triumph came with Ajax now regarded as one of the best sides in Europe and the world. Cruyff, Rep and Neeskins were household names. Their third European Cup Final in a row saw them face Italian giants Juventus. Johnny Rep scored the winning goal with a great looping header in Belgrade.

Cruyff must've been becoming sick of the annual classic photo shot of him, coming off the plane nonchalantly holding the European Cup aloft. When he casually strolled down the steps in 1973 it would prove to be the last time he won the trophy as a player. Ajax had joined a select group of clubs to have achieved three European cup titles in a row.

There were problems behind the scenes for Cruyff though, and after his team-mates voted him out as captain, within three weeks he left Ajax to live and work in Catalonia.

Chapter 12

1974 World Cup and That Turn

BY THE 1974 World Cup finals in West Germany, Cruyff was one of the biggest football stars in the world. Thousands of great players have graced the tournament throughout the decades and made it there based on their play, skill, goals, and their profile but only an elite few have something extra that elevates them to another level. Sócrates, Zico, Zidane, and of course Cruyff are on that list.

Leading into the tournament, Johan Cruyff had won three consecutive European Cups in 1971, 1972, and 1973. He had been subject to one of the biggest transfer fees in the history of the game, six million guilders, just under $2m, or £929,000, in a move from Ajax to Barcelona. He had led Barca to their first LaLiga title since 1960, and in one game he recalibrated the balance of power in Spanish football when he starred as his side trounced Real Madrid 5-0.

Tactically the Dutch appeared ready. Cruyff had even convinced Rinus Michels that the last piece of the Total Football jigsaw had to be sorted – the need for a goalkeeper who came off his line. Jan ver Beveren was then the most famous and successful goalkeeper the Dutch had. He starred for Sparta Rotterdam and PSV Eindhoven, playing over 400 times combined for both sides. He was the recognised number one and regarded as a wonderful shot-stopper who stayed on his line. However, when they headed to West Germany for the 1974 World Cup finals, Cruyff convinced Michels he should include Jan Jongbloed in the team. Jongbloed was regarded as more of a maverick and somewhat eccentric. He was also older, yet Cruyff persuaded Michels that Jongbloed was great with the ball at his feet, and in his youth, was a great striker who wasn't afraid to play it from the back. Since ver Beveren preferred to stay on his line, and a sweeper-keeper was a huge advantage to any side considering playing Total Football, Cruyff had his way.

With a goalkeeper playing as a defender, suddenly the possibilities opened up. The Dutch could press higher, and they did, only conceded one goal prior to the final and almost winning the World Cup. It's commonplace now and many coaches insist on having goalkeepers who are comfortable playing football outside the box.

This World Cup had something distinctive about it. This was a brave new world – and why wouldn't it be, with that German efficiency and organisation. When they suggested the world was watching they meant it. Games were beamed to 91 countries; the organisers estimated a potential viewing audience of between 400 and 600 million would be watching each game.

It was on this backdrop of a high-profile competition that Cruyff, already an international superstar, did something instinctive which confirmed his position in the pantheon of football history as a true great. He performed what became known as the 'Cruyff Turn', and as the world was watching, he sent millions of kids into emergency wards across the globe who tried to copy him and ended up doing themselves an injury.

Swedish defender Jan Olsson may have been left looking like a drunk Keystone Cop, chasing the bank robbers the wrong way down a one-way street on to oncoming traffic. Or the hapless idiots you see desperately careering, in a rudderless kayak, toward a sheer drop down a 300ft waterfall masquerading as a ravine.

The moment that gave birth to the turn occurred in the 23rd minute of a Group 3 match against Sweden, in the Westfalenstadion in Dortmund. The Dutch are playing it, shuffling and dancing, seemingly in perpetual motion. This is Total Football. Wim van Hanegem is pressured by two Swedes on the right wing, but he manages to keep possession by feeding Wim Rijsbergen. But where's Cruyff? Is that him over on the left wing? What's he doing over there? Why is Piet Keizer not there? I don't understand this (I'm eight years old). Rijsbergen moves it inside to Arie Haan, who takes a few steps, sets himself up, then launches a lengthy diagonal pass. Is this supposed to be wonderful, flowing football?

Cruyff sees the ball coming and stretches to control the pass with his left foot. Olsson marks Cruyff tightly. Cruyff is now facing his own half and looks like he is about to pass the ball back and keep play circulating by feeding in the left-sided midfielder. This is when one of the most important parts of the move happens.

While Olsson follows the ball, Cruyff continues with the ruse, feigning a pass before bringing his right foot back as though to play the ball but instead throws a dummy which fools Olsson. Cruyff's body opens up then his foot caresses the top of the ball, before he pulls it back and in behind his left leg. He quickly spins through 180 degrees, shifting the balance of his weight to the other foot. Bang! Cruyff quickly flips around. He executed a 180-degree turn with the ball – leaving his marker looking hapless and lost. How is that even possible? Is he double-jointed?

Cruyff could have hospitalised himself, the way he twisted his hips. He flipped the balance of his weight on to his left and then scarpered into the Swedish 18-yard box. He then played an average cross with the outside of his right foot; a signature technique used throughout his career, when he played for Ajax against Celtic in Glasgow, and on countless occasions when he played for Feyenoord. The cross came to Rep but he couldn't get it under control. Van Hanegem tried to take it on but didn't manage to get a shot away.

It is airbrushed out of the 'Cruyff Turn' story but nothing came of this defining moment of the player's career. Such a wondrous display of balletic poise, which everyone raves about, was merely a showboating exercise. Yes, it's one of the most audacious pieces of skill ever displayed on a football pitch, but there was no end product.

For football purists, what's most noticeable about the move is the position Cruyff finds himself in when he brings the ball out of the air. Cruyff is out of position on the left wing where Keizer should be (he and Johnny Rep had a nightmare of a game). Perhaps if it had been Keizer who crossed the ball in then Cruyff would've got a shot away, at least forcing the keeper to make a save.

The game ended 0-0 and Sweden were unlucky not to sneak it. It is noticeable how hard the Dutch pressed the Swedes while trying to play their Total Football. At times, as many as seven players hunt down a Swedish player with the ball. In the last ten minutes, though, Sweden had two chances. Roland Sandberg blew one from close range and Edström had a shot cleared by Arie Haan. The Swedish keeper with the fabulous name, Ronnie Hellström, played one of those matches – tell me there's a heavy metal band in Sweden called Hellström and if not, why not? The Dutch side couldn't get the ball past him. They still finished top and the Swedes qualified in second place and advanced to the second group stage. Cruyff was unhappy but remained pragmatic, 'It is a pity when you fail to produce a positive result after playing so well. We have played attacking and entertaining football.' Yes, but you couldn't score a goal.

The amiable defender Olsson's biggest mistake was to mark the best player in the world, playing at the peak of his powers. Olsson readily accepted and delights in still talking about it. He could only marvel at the famous move and is anything but embarrassed by it. As a pro, he appreciated the level of skill and technique on show. Olsson still acts with grace and delight. He explains he was older, 32, and admittedly out of his depth when he was left mesmerised by the 'Cruyff Turn'. When commenting in 2020, Olsson's thoughts remained clear. 'My team-mates after the game, we looked at each other, they started to laugh and I did the same, I laughed then and I laugh now,' Olsson told the PA news agency. 'It was very funny. He was a world-class player. I did my best, but I was not a world-class player.'

The famous Cruyff Turn would prove to be a mere starter in the incredible feast of scintillating football served up by the Dutch, and their star, during that World Cup. In their semi-final they had an ominous challenge against world champions Brazil. Cruyff was looking forward to it and remained unfazed, 'The big game was against Brazil, the world champions, that was really the game everyone was focused on. We didn't only outplay the Brazilians, but we outplayed them with the best football. We played football the world loved.' When they couldn't keep up with the Dutch movement or skill, the Brazilians got physical and dirty. The Netherlands reached the final with a 2-0 win because they could play like that too. Remember, for Total Football to work, your side had to leave the boot in and get physical when required.

Cruyff's second goal against Brazil is often held up as the template, the benchmark goal that encapsulates the essence of Total Football. It was also voted goal of the tournament. Winning goals are often spectacular wonder strikes from 35 yards out, overhead kicks, or remarkable volleys. While Cruyff's stretching near-post volley was superb, this goal of the tournament was an acceptance that goals can be judged on their build-up, fluidity and interplay. The Dutch were now famous – their style of play had beaten the Brazilians, and they were on their way to the final to meet the hosts West Germany.

There was something dramatic, clear and vivid about the contrast in style, attitude and even colour to the final. The game itself would perpetuate the familiar and well-trodden narrative; the Dutch won hearts, playing with a swashbuckling, attacking style, but West Germany won the trophy. The Germans didn't get the credit they deserved, and any they did get was granted grudgingly. West Germany, with a vast array of wonderful players, were instead held up as party poopers. The question was, 'How could they have beaten the rightful winners?' Well, the answer was simple. They beat the Netherlands in the final.

This Dutch side would be regarded as the best team to have never won the World Cup, behind the Brazil side of 1982, featuring Sócrates, Zico, Falcão and Éder. Zico technically was perfect; great with his left and right foot, a dead ball expert, he had everything except a little funny thing above his name like every other legend I've mentioned. Then, oh yes, there was the Puskás Hungary side of 1954. So, apart from those.

As for the competition itself, we often hear pundits and commentators suggesting teams like Italy and Germany, former champions, play their way into a tournament and that was true in this case, as the hosts navigated their way to the final. The first group section saw a 1-0 win over Chile, an expected 3-0 victory over Australia but a loss to East Germany (this was the only competitive game ever between the two sides). The West Germans finished in second position. In the semi-final group they improved with dogged performances over Yugoslavia, then a trouncing of Sweden and a dour and resolute victory over a tough Poland.

The Dutch, on the other hand, beat Uruguay 2-0, drew 0-0 in the 'Cruyff Turn' game with Sweden, then beat Bulgaria 4-1. In the semi-final group, they raised their game again, beating Argentina 4-0, then defeating both East Germany and Brazil 2-0.

My favourite moment of the 1974 World Cup, when watching as a kid, might be a slightly unusual one. It was when the Dutch players passed it back and forth to each other in the first minute of the final, like a group of friends meeting over the park for a Sunday afternoon kick-about. They kicked off the game playing at walking pace, nonchalantly moving the ball around. As I watched, I had the feeling everyone across the globe would be complaining about the Dutch, assuming it was yet another drab, boring, World Cup Final.

The sky was overcast, rain was in the air, and even the ball, the classic black-and-white-panelled Adidas Telstar Durlast 1974, seemed aesthetically pleasing on the eye. The Dutch appeared to be circulating the ball around to let each other get a touch. While the ball was passed around at a slow pace, off it the Dutch side continually moved. They kept possession for a reason. It did not look like it, but there was a purpose. Cruyff came back into his half, took a pass, upped the tempo, played it wide with a little more intensity and there was a subtle change in shape.

West Germany were still bedding in, working out positions and who they should be marking in a constant interchanging conveyor belt that was the Clockwork Orange system. They had yet to even touch the ball when, suddenly, Cruyff received possession. He was inside the West German half and ran directly at them. The solo run was deliberate, measured and targeted. He pressed through the middle, opening up the play. He saw a gap but kept the ball and powered into the heart of the

West German defence. Berti Vogts tried to pick up Cruyff but he found another gear and burst between Vogts and Hoeneß. When Cruyff was brought down by Hoeneß, a penalty was awarded by English referee Jack Taylor. It was the first minute of the 1974 World Cup Final and Cruyff had won his team a golden opportunity from the spot.

Johan Neeskens stepped up to take the kick. When German goalkeeper Sepp Maier moved a fraction too early, making it clear he was going to the right, Neeskens walloped the penalty straight and hard down the middle. When the goal was scored, not one German player had touched the ball. Amid the celebrations, Cruyff was the most cautious, telling his team-mates to calm down and stay focused. He knew it was too perfect a start.

Due to their performances throughout the competition and their style of play, the Dutch side had endeared themselves to the neutral. They were the flying Dutchmen and nothing would stop them now. These bohemian hipsters were like a rock band on tour; long-haired, carefree artists, rattling their love beads in the scintillating and balmy heat. Then there was the football, too. The script was going to plan. This was their moment and the Dutch superstars were on their way.

But for Cruyff, Rep and Neeskens, the Germans could hold up Beckenbauer, Breitner and Müller. Cruyff was a huge fan of the West German captain Franz Beckenbauer. Tonny Bruins Slot, who would later be Cruyff's assistant coach at Ajax and Barcelona, was unequivocal about Cruyff's love of Beckenbauer, 'Cruyff was crazy for Beckenbauer at Germany and Bayern Munich, because he'd move from the back into midfield to gain an advantage in that line.'

Cruyff knew the Germans were tough opponents and would respond. They had a history of turning it around in the final and knew how to win. He may have already been drawing parallels with Hungary, in 1954's 'Miracle of Berne' when the West German side, then still playing in a league not fully professional, dashed the hopes and dreams of Puskás and his side's 36-match unbeaten run. Hungary, like the Dutch, were the people's favourites. West German coach Sepp Herberger had moulded a well-drilled, tight-knit band of brothers, up against Hungary, a team of great individual players. This was the game which spawned Herberger's famous quote, 'The ball is round, the game lasts 90 minutes. Everything else is pure theory.'

As his team-mates celebrated and jogged back to the halfway line, Cruyff knew the early goal would have upset the opposition. They had to close the game down and finish them off. Cruyff also knew his team wouldn't resist the chance to play to their growing number of admirers on the biggest stage of all. They started to show off and play to the gallery. For some unforgivable reason, the Dutch were deliberately trying to demean their opponents instead of going for a second goal. Perhaps it was their maverick, liberal approach? Cruyff's men made the mistake of toying with the Germans.

It's too easy to say the West Germans' mentality was one of their strongest characteristics. It is grossly unfair to the array of world-class talent they had to lay that cliché on them. They were also the reigning European champions. In the subsequent major competition, the 1976 Euros, they narrowly lost out in the final to that famous penalty by Czechoslovakia's Antonín

Panenka. They showed more than a resolute mentality. When they won the ball they made great use of it.

The Germans fought back and in the 25th minute, Wim Jansen gave away a soft penalty when Bernd Hölzenbein dived over his leg. Breitner subsequently scored from the spot. Breitner himself was a great case study of someone playing something close to Total Football. He started as a powerful right-footed striker, then became a left-back who liked to maraud into midfield and score goals. He was as much a Total Football expert as anyone in the Dutch side. His goal against Chile in the opening game saw the left-back shoot from over 35 yards out, on the right-hand side, after some fluid German interplay. Were West Germany playing Total Football but not receiving any credit for it?

Gerd Müller, arguably one of the finest goalscorers to have ever lived, netted just before half-time to make it 2-1 when he managed to control the ball and tougher still, maintain his balance, to cut back a great right-footed shot past Jongbloed. The Dutch had chance after chance to equalise; many squandered or saved by Maier. But Germany had opportunities too; in the second half Müller scored a great goal only for it to be disallowed, and Hölzenbein was again brought down in the box for what looked like a clear penalty but on this occasion, the decision was not given. To the disappointment of their many new fans around the world, the game ended 2-1 with West Germany lifting the World Cup.

Decades later Cruyff would have time to reflect, 'I think we played with a little too much confidence. We missed such a lot of chances. So we played quite well but the details were not there and you saw it in too many small different details and one of those was scoring goals.' Party animal Johnny Rep was more succinct, 'We really had a great time there. We forgot we had to win.'

Let's go back to the turn and hear from Jan Olsson, who has a wonderful attitude about the predicament he found himself in and thinks about it every day. Not in a mournful and regretful way, and even after having time to reflect, Olsson does so with great clarity of thought, 'I thought I was going to take the ball. I still cannot understand. Now when I see the video, every time, I think I have got the ball. When he is about to kick the ball, I am sure I am going to take it, but every time he surprises me. I loved everything about this moment.'

He doesn't have photographs or mementoes, 'I have the memory. It is a moment I remember every day. Every day I think about football, I think about Johan Cruyff. I had the pleasure to meet him – a great player, great coach, great gentleman, I think he had everything.' Olsson sought out and congratulated Cruyff after the game. Perhaps the greatest lesson to come from the 1974 finals wasn't Cruyff's turn, but the humility and grace shown by Olsson.

Olsson's modesty serves to merely confirm what any real football fan and mere mortal would be like. He was lucky enough to represent his country and faced the best player in the world, at his peak. His reaction to being the player Cruyff turned is as inspirational as the move itself. What a wonderful gentleman.

Cruyff's turn elevated his career and was a wonderful moment for football. It was one of the most inspirational moments of individual brilliance, and it caught and captivated a global audience. The turn was one of the defining moments of Cruyff's career. Total Football had the world engrossed but in the end, the swashbuckling style and flair may have thrilled but only resulted in a runners-up medal. The Dutch won the hearts, and Cruyff was the player of the tournament, but West Germany won the trophy.

Apart from the turn, there's the Cruyff Institute. Ajax renamed their stadium in his honour to the Johan Cruijff ArenA. He also has a distant planet named after him, which began with the number 14 and was known as '14282', until it was renamed 'Cruijff' (it's a minor planet, an asteroid, and is about nine kilometres in diameter and takes a total of five years, three months and 18 days to journey around the sun). How appropriate for a player who, at times, was out of this world. I always think he would've loved that.

Young Johan
checks out an Alfa
Romeo in 1968.

June 1971,
becoming a young
idol.

Relaxing at Wembley the day before the 1971 European Cup Final. Ajax beat Panathinaikos 2-0.

Cruyff and Inter Milan's Gabriele Oriali, 1972 European Cup Final. Cruyff scored both in the 2-0 win, held in De Kuip, Rotterdam.

In the 1973 final, Ajax beat Juventus 1-0 to win their third European Cup in a row. After the players deposed him as captain, he signed for Barcelona.

Cruyff signed for Barcelona in August 1973. He teamed up with his mentor, Rinus Michels, at the Nou Camp.

Cruyff endeared himself to the Catalan cause by arguing with authority. Here, police escort him off the field, in a home defeat to Malaga.

Argentina in the 1974 World Cup, Cruyff dribbles past goalkeeper Daniel Carnevali to score on 26 June 1974 in Gelsenkirchen, popularising Total Football and staying on his feet, learned from the concrete streets of Betondorp.

Cruyff wins a penalty in the first minute of the 1974 World Cup Final.

Cruyff retires, here joking with Sepp Maier before a farewell game on 7 November 1978 against Bayern. The German side did not adhere to friendly rules, walloping Ajax 8-0.

Playing soccer for the New York Cosmos. Cruyff did not like AstroTurf and signed for LA Aztecs.

1978 at the LA Aztecs. Cruyff teamed up again with Rinus Michels and was named the league's MVP.

With the Washington Dips and hanging out with the Kennedys.

Back in Europe, at Ajax, his agent arranged a cut of gate receipts. Here up against a young Louis van Gaal of Sparta Rotterdam.

At Feyenoord, Cruyff took over the team's tactics, positioning and shape. He also coached while playing. Here in the UEFA Cup, Hoddle stole the show.

Playing away games, the stadiums were mostly sell-outs like this one at Go Ahead Eagles.

Cruyff and Gullit hold up the KNVB Beker (the Dutch Cup) at the double-winning civic reception in Rotterdam.

Cruyff became Barcelona coach in May 1988 and noticed a disconnect between fans and club and opened training to fans. He often watched training sitting on a ball claiming mistakes were easier to spot.

Cruyff was made honorary president at Barcelona in 2010 but was ousted by the incoming president, Sandro Rosell.

Excelling as a football pundit and a columnist in De Telegraaf, his hard hitting opinions sparked the Velvet Revolution at Ajax.

Chapter 13

Cruyff Live in the Flesh, the Dutch Beatle

IF EYEWITNESS proof were required of the astonishing standard and level Cruyff was playing at months before he was dismissed by Ajax and headed to Feyenoord, call me as a witness.

On 15 September 1982, along with 56,298 fans, I saw Johan Cruyff play in the flesh; it's a memory and experience I treasure. He played for Ajax against Celtic, at Celtic Park, in the first round of the European Cup. I was 16 and watched him play in what would turn out to be his final season for Ajax. If Cruyff's level of consistency had dipped it didn't show. He was still a pivotal part of the team. He played in a deeper role yet still covered an astonishing amount of ground. One of Cruyff's mantras is about how a Dutch player can touch the ball only once and know where to run. When I watched him play, that's exactly what he did; one touch, and run into space.

I was excited from the moment I woke up. I couldn't concentrate at school. For me, Cruyff was the football equivalent of a Beatle. He was the coolest footballer ever. Pelé and Maradona are fantastic individuals but Johan Cruyff was their equal individually and in my mind, an even better team player and tactician. Cruyff's greatness was achieved not as an individual, but within the difficult confines of the team. I couldn't take my eyes off him the whole game and he controlled it, moving and playing with amazing mathematical fluidity.

Cruyff was a product of his time. Sophisticated, controversial, stylish, opinionated, he embodied each decade, from flower power to revolution, to glam rock, to social unrest, to punk, to new wave, then even more social struggle and revolution. Here was someone who had not only played but starred, over three decades, at the highest level. He was like the Beatles and the Stones, the Sex Pistols and the Clash, the Human League and Joy Division and had transcended every aspect of culture in its broadest manifestation; art, film, theatre. From peace and love to post-industrial landscapes, glam rock to punk, to the 1980s of miners' strikes and football hooliganism. But always there, always playing, always instigating, always smiling and always complaining, he remained one step ahead. By the time you'd thought it, he'd done it. Now, here he was, in front of me. In the flesh.

The pedantic football fan in me hadn't thought this through. I confess to being slightly upset when Ajax ran out of the tunnel in their blue away strip. It was like an Everton strip, featuring blue shorts with blue and white socks. I was genuinely disappointed not to see the iconic white and red Ajax jersey. Cruyff wasn't even wearing the number 14 shirt; instead, he wore the number nine. This was like watching Brazil play in their blue away strip. It isn't Brazil, is it? Celtic were in the hoops. For once, I would've been happy to see my team play in their away shirt. It didn't look right showing up to see Cruyff's Ajax in a blue shirt. Once he started running and directing play I forgot about the classic red and white kit.

If Johan is listening, somewhere out in the great beyond, I must apologise, as I was sneaked into the game. I got what is known as a 'lift-over' the turnstiles to see you play. Though quite why at 6ft 1in aged 16, I had the cheek to still ask someone to help carry me over the turnstiles is a mystery to me. I wanted to contribute to the club but my financial situation came into play. It was an all-ticket game too. How I was allowed to do it, I still don't know but in those days the official attendance was always way off. This was often the way in this era of football, with grounds tightly packed and overcrowded.

That evening it rained, not heavily but the kind of clinging, thin and continuous rain that made you wet. It was smeary, one of those wet autumnal Scottish evenings, under floodlights. Nature's perfect backdrop for a dramatic night like this. Flashbulbs from cameras would go off in the crowd, mostly from the posh seats in the main stand, every time Cruyff had a touch of the ball. When he took a throw-in it was like a lightning storm. It was like Beatlemania or a film star arriving at a premiere. Seriously.

I had the strangest thought too, before kick-off. Imagine playing for Celtic against Cruyff, and having a chance to tell people you shared the same field as him. I was nervous watching him, so I can't imagine what the team must have felt like. Maybe they'd be determined to impress Cruyff? How early in the game would it be appropriate to ask if he would swap shirts?

The night's four goals came inside the first 29 minutes. When Ajax scored early, the crowd turned deadly silent. Cruyff looked slightly smaller and thinner than I expected. He looked wiry. But I did notice he had long legs. I know this sounds peculiar but it's what I thought. When I say to people Cruyff had long legs, they laugh. Years later, I remember reading Hugh McIlvanney describing Cruyff. This was at a relaxed press conference before the World Cup Final in 1974. McIlvanney would, as any great writer should, survey, study and describe the player.

In an article in the *Observer*, on meeting Cruyff, he wrote, 'Cruyff has more than his status as one of the finest of contemporary footballers to make him an immensely attractive figure.' McIlvanney could've been a detective, forensically detailing and weighing up a possible suspect. 'His physique, like his play, is made up of sharp edges rather than curves. The face is small, thin and fresher than his 27 years should have left it with only the slightest stubble fighting through on an unaggressive chin.' You can imagine the writer puffing on a cigar as he continues to sum up the measure of the man, the legend in front of him. 'Even scuffing in loose slippers through the public rooms of the Wald Hotel at Hiltrup, exchanging pleasantries with the Dutch reporters who have chronicled his rise since his days as a schoolboy prodigy in Amsterdam, he moves on those extraordinary long legs with a contained unaffected grace.'

Considering it was eight hard years later for Cruyff, it was uncanny to compare McIlvanney's opinion to what I saw, 'On the field, he is as straight and incisive as a knife. His physical skills (electrifying pace and control, flawlessly crisp striking of the ball) and his absolute awareness of where the areas of danger and opportunity lie at any moment, enable him to organise and build superbly in deep positions and to materialise in front of goal with interventions that are as final as death.'

In front of me, right there, Johan Cruyff, with the same mannerisms when he passed and moved and the long sleeves, the sprint within a sprint. At 35, he should've been doing less but seemed to be everywhere. One of those GPS stat checkers the modern player wears would have read 12km easily.

Cruyff did something directly in front of us in the Jungle, the terracing enclosure directly across from the Main Stand. He played a pass with the outside of his right foot, from the left wing. It appears to have a name, although I hadn't heard of it. He played a 'trivela'. I don't like this word as it sounds too modern, like a type of hipster pizza, or a food delivery company, or a skateboard flip. He played a 'trivela' pass and crossed to his team-mate 60 yards away in the box. The ball was perfectly weighted, finding his team-mate for the header.

Everyone breathed in, then exhaled, then without thinking, applauded, respect where it was due. That was genius. That was Cruyff. One of those moments when you're at a football game and partisanship slips, your opponent does something breathtaking and at once, simultaneously, without thinking, the crowd applauds. Cruyff glimpsed quickly, a half-second, toward the Jungle, at the applause from the crowd, shrugged, rolled his eyes and gave a slight, rueful smile and ran on.

Wow. Cruyff bossed it. He ordered and coached and talked and cajoled and pointed and ran and paused and turned.

He twisted, tackled, shouted, argued, veered, applauded, encouraged. And this was without the ball. When he did have it, he was magical. He would initiate moves deep and through some Einstein-Cruyff-Euclid equation appear elsewhere, knowing the ball would be there. Oh and as well as being hugely influential in the shape of the game, he refereed it too. Every kick, every play, he officiated.

Like a mathematical conman and trickster, Cruyff would always be able to find another angle. Not only could he play brilliantly with both feet, he was tremendous at heading and had a wonderful pass in him. He had the intelligence to match his skill. He always had a tremendous overview of the game with sensational vision.

It was evident when you saw him play that football was a process about distance, closing down, and using space. Defending meant not giving your opponent time. Bizarrely, Cruyff thought football, or at least how he played it, was about having a sixth sense. His colleagues at Ajax and then the Netherlands had been drilled so much on how to do their work, it became second nature. It was about instinct. When discussing this, he cited a goal he scored against ADO Den Haag in 1969 as an example. As he fixed his socks, tying tape to them, he saw the ball being cleared to him on the left. He controlled it in a half volley and the ball's natural arc spun it around his opponent. As he turned and because it was still spinning, in one movement, he curved it over the goalkeeper into the net. One touch and a shot. Goal. It was sheer instinct. If he had taken the time to think about it, it may not have happened or at least not with the same fluency. This goal encapsulated the razor-sharp instinct of the elite footballer in that split-second, when such shows of skill were merely a reflex action. These brief glimpses of a quick and alert mind separate the top professional footballers from the sport's superstars. They have done their 10,000 hours, practised their technique, their touch, then there are the players on a higher plane who react without thinking about it.

In the game itself, despite two chances in the opening minutes, missed by Frank McGarvey, it was Ajax's Dane, Jesper Olsen, who drew first blood. He drove, veered and twisted around the Celtic defence like they were statues and got past Davie Moyes before rocketing the ball between Pat Bonner and his near post. There were only four minutes gone.

In the 12th minute, Ajax's replacement keeper Hans Galjé (having stepped in for Piet Schrijvers, who was injured in the warm-up) made a great save from a 30-yard Davie Provan free kick. When Provan caught the Ajax defence sleeping, with the sort of quick thinking Cruyff was famed for, and played a quick pass from the corner to Tommy Burns in the box, the star man tackled and brought down Burns. It was weak but the decision was correct. The penalty was coolly finished by Charlie Nicholas.

Olsen wreaked havoc throughout the game and Celtic couldn't get to grips with him. Three minutes after Celtic brought the game level, Olsen again tore down the left and chipped inside to Cruyff who deftly jabbed a cushioned pass on to Ajax's captain, Søren Lerby, who stayed cool and neatly chipped it into the net.

Celtic thought they had scored when Tommy Burns looped in a free kick and the Ajax defence failed to clear their lines.

Nicholas was quick to latch on, round the keeper and score but the goal wasn't given.

When Galjé briefly forgot about Total Football and fell into the trap of playing the less refined Scottish game, his launch was met with a superb headed clearance from Moyes. This found Nicholas whose flicked header created confusion between Leo van Veen and his goalie. Frank McGarvey reacted quickest to put it under the advancing keeper and equalise at 2-2. This would be the last goal of the night.

In the second half, the game settled down and there were clear chances early on when Nicholas was through, and later Celtic had a penalty claim dismissed when Burns was again brought down in the box. As the game closed out, Bonner pulled off an incredible save from Lerby. It was remarkable to see Ajax take the heat and sting out of the match and settle for the draw.

The game was widely recognised, up until then at least, as among the most exciting, end-to-end European ties played at Celtic Park. Even the sanest Hoops fan would concur that they were out having conceded two home goals to a better side who looked like, if they needed to, they could find another level. The newspapers were unanimous in feeling that Celtic's hopes hung by a thread thanks to a Danish double and Dutch masterclass from Cruyff. Ajax's two away goals left the Scottish side's qualification near impossible. Manager Billy McNeill went through the motions, telling the press they would face a huge challenge in Amsterdam but in football anything is possible. Ajax boss Aad de Mos was confident they had done more than enough and had been pictured celebrating the draw with Cruyff like a victory.

Celtic, as is often the case, didn't stick to the script and won the second leg with goals from Nicholas and George McCluskey, taking them through to the next round where they would face Real Sociedad after a 4-3 scoreline. After the match, when a nervous McCluskey chapped the door of the Ajax dressing room to ask if anyone wanted to swap jerseys, he was met with stony silence. But as he turned to leave the dressing room, crestfallen and slightly embarrassed, Cruyff, who was receiving treatment on the massage table, shouted, 'McCluskey – I'll swap with you. Well played.'

Throughout his career, Cruyff was often accused of being spiky and arrogant and off-hand with opponents, yet at Celtic Park at the end of the first leg, as Ajax headed off, he brought back his team to the centre circle and made them applaud and salute and wave to the crowd to say thanks.

After the defeat in the 1974 World Cup Final, he stood and shook hands and embraced his German opponents as they stepped up to receive the trophy. It's rarely shown on TV but seconds after the game was finished, Cruyff does something most players couldn't. He warmly congratulates them and the West Germans thank him back. They don't make footballers or football teams like that anymore. Johan Cruyff was class.

Chapter 14

Season 1983/84: Matchdays 14–23

FOR MATCHDAY 14, Feyenoord welcomed newly promoted DS'79. A side with a long history, set up in 1883, as Dordrechtsche Football Club (DFC), they are now known as FC Dordrecht. They would be relegated again at the end of the season.

They do, however, have the honour of being subject to a great trivia fact – Johan Cruyff played for them in three friendlies in January 1981. The home side took the game to Schapenkoppen (the sheep heads) from the off. The first goal came from a corner with Peter Houtman driving home a powerful left-footed shot in the ninth minute for his seventh goal of the season. DS'79 equalised after some neat build-up play in the 23rd minute when Jaap van der Wiel broke through to neatly slot away from inside the box. The striker's change of pace and movement resembled Johan Cruyff. In the second half, a late tackle gave Feyenoord a free kick on the right. Cruyff delivered a superb cross and Gullit headed home the winner. DS'79 were hardly a box office pull and the crowd was a disappointing 19,213.

Feyenoord next headed to FC Utrecht, in the centre of the Netherlands, to take on the fourth-placed side. A crowd of 19,000 showed up on a Baltic day to witness this revitalised Feyenoord team with Cruyff at the helm. Historically, Utrecht used to be the most important city in the Netherlands until the Dutch golden age, when it was overtaken by Amsterdam.

This particular game saw two Dutch greats, one from the past and one who would bring back glory, and most importantly win something for the Dutch in the future, score both the goals. It ended 2-0 to the visitors with a tenth-minute goal from Gullit, his sixth of the season, and a 39th-minute goal from Cruyff, his fifth. Interestingly, Utrecht midfielders Dick Advocaat and Jan Wouters would evolve into a successful managerial double act.

Matchday 16, and December in Rotterdam is hardly a time for slapping on the sun-blocker and shades, perhaps explaining the low turnout to see Willem II come to town. Only 16,170 hardy souls witnessed a comfortable 4-0 win for Feyenoord. There were several issues including a midday kick-off, Sunday service for transport and just three weeks until Christmas. Andrey Zhelyaskov scored the opener after 28 minutes but it took a second-half hat-trick from Peter Houtman to seal the victory, taking his goals scored tally for the season to ten.

On matchday 17 Feyenoord headed to the city and municipality of Zwolle in the north-east of the country to take on Zwolle '82 (Zwolle would go into bankruptcy, returning as FC Zwolle, in 1990 – and be renamed again in 2012 as PEC Zwolle). A crowd of 15,000 that turned out to see the high flyers would have been glad that they had. It had looked like a huge shock was on the cards with the visitors trailing 2-0 at half-time. Zwolle were on form, playing well and sitting in fifth position in the Eredivisie. They were one of those sides who, especially at home in a rammed stadium, were more than capable of forcing a title run off the rails. They scored after seven minutes with a Gerard van Moorst goal. In the season of goodwill, their second came from a Gullit own goal in the 32nd minute. In the second half, Feyenoord came out fighting. Houtman's 11th goal of the season made it 2-1 and it was left to the reliable André Stafleu to equalise in the 87th minute and keep their unbeaten run going. This game saw Cruyff face former Ajax and Netherlands team-mate Johnny Rep, playing up front for Zwolle. It was a dropped point but Feyenoord remained on a ten-game unbeaten run since their defeat to Ajax.

With the first half of the season over for Cruyff and Feyenoord, they didn't have much time to rest on their laurels. A quick look at the mid-term report card would show the first round of 17 games yielded 13 wins, three draws and one defeat. That particular loss might have felt catastrophic but it was, after all, only two points. They were at the top of the league.

Now they had to take this form into the second half of the season and on matchday 18, they faced FC Volendam, who were lying 15th in the league, at De Kuip. The crowd was low, with only 14,702 diehard fans attending. Still, it was January, Christmas was a recent memory, and the game was not one for the purists. Those there would see Gullit score after ten minutes and midway through the second half, Cruyff made it 2-0 with his sixth goal of the season.

Midway through the season, Cruyff had instigated a change in the team. The fans' favourite, the experienced left-winger Pierre Vermeulen, was dropped and in his place came Stanley Brard. Cruyff liked Stan's energy and power. He was only on a part-time contract, training twice a week and was a PE teacher, super fit, and had an incredible engine. The left-back became a left-winger, doing Cruyff's running for him. Brard was cutting off the supply in the face of the opposition's full-back, playing much further up the park and along with Ben Wijnstekers powering up and down the wing, Cruyff could get further up the park, and do less running back. Stan would be able to get back when Feyenoord lost the ball and Cruyff was able to rest, and do more damage. The setup was always the same, a fluid 4-3-3, and it was working.

The show was next on the road to face Helmond Sport. A 7,000 crowd jammed in tight to watch a convincing 5-0 win. Stafleu opened the scoring with a sixth-minute goal, and Hoekstra scored four minutes later to make it 2-0. Only ten minutes had passed and Helmond looked out of the game. When Houtman gave Feyenoord the third goal after 24 minutes, it was done and dusted. Stanley Brard scored his first goal of the season after 71 minutes, shortly before Gullit was replaced by Mario Been, who got on the scoresheet with the fifth goal. The future coach in Cruyff would've been reminding his team-mates that this was a Total Football scoreline. The goals were spread throughout the team from five individual players.

Next up, a curious and impressive 15,000 crowd showed up to watch Fortuna Sittard host Feyenoord to see one of the finest players their nation had ever produced. Feyenoord took the lead when Sjaak Troost scored with a great left-footed shot from outside the box, his first of the season. When Fortuna didn't clear their lines André Hoekstra pounced to drive home the second from six yards in the 11th minute. Gullit created the third with a simple pass to Hoekstra then Cruyff played in Gullit with two minutes to go for 4-0.

On matchday 21, Feyenoord welcomed 12th-placed Den Bosch. A crowd of 19,500 witnessed the Rotterdammers wobble and stumble with the game ending 1-1. Feyenoord scored first through André Stafleu on 24 minutes. Den Bosch levelled before half-time with Wim van der Horst getting on the scoresheet. It should've been a win but the draw meant Feyenoord's unbeaten run since the humbling by Ajax now stood at 14 games. The wily Cruyff would no doubt remind everyone in the dressing room at full time that this was consistent and impressive championship-winning form. The home fans were reluctantly starting to dream as the Cruyff bandwagon rolled on.

Sixth-placed Haarlem visited the league leaders for matchday 22 but the side were still sleeping in the early stages. Feyenoord took the lead in the first minute with yet another goal coming from Hoekstra, who scored again in the sixth minute. The game was over when Hoekstra bagged an impressive hat-trick after half an hour. Feyenoord's coach Thijs Libregts nodded his head sagely as he must've sensed something special was in the air this season. Haarlem's Hans van Doorneveld must have been pulling his hair out.

Van Doorneveld's half-time hairdryer treatment kept Feyenoord at bay for a total of six minutes. In the 51st minute, Gullit made it four. Leading comfortably and cruising,

Feyenoord took off Cruyff in the 59th minute. What could go wrong? Well, Haarlem scored twice in quick succession through Edwin van Hameren in the 63rd minute and Wim Balm in the 67th. Normal service was resumed when Gullit scored two minutes later to make it 5-2. Libregts must've breathed easier when a Chris Verkaik own goal made it 6-2 before Gullit sealed his hat-trick in the final minute to make it 7-2. It was a tale of two halves, and two hat-tricks, in front of a disappointing crowd of 16,519.

Feyenoord, confident and playing well, took their unbeaten run to face Groningen on matchday 23. On the face of it, this should have been a routine game.

This was the best side in the league, on form, with Hoekstra, Gullit and Houtman (but no Cruyff), facing the side sitting in sixth position. From footage of this game, you immediately have a sense of how cold it is. The teams had the fresh-faced expression of a bracing chill and cold wind. If they stayed stationary too long, they would be shivering and hypothermia would soon kick in. However, it was terrible witnessing players wearing tracksuit bottoms, and one player wore white gloves. White gloves? Seriously? Leave the white gloves to Mickey Mouse, mate.

The second thing you notice is no Cruyff. Cruyff's substitution against Haarlem must've been more than a precautionary measure and he was absent for the only time that season. When he didn't play, Feyenoord were beaten. One league game out of the side tells you everything you need to know about Cruyff's influence. In Ruud Gullit's book, *How to Watch Football*, he elucidates: 'It was not the manager [Thijs

143

Libregts] but Cruyff who dictated tactics and positions. My place in his ideal Feyenoord line-up was as a pure outside-right. Once again, a whole new situation to adapt to, but Cruyff's will was law.'

With the game all square going into the second half, Groningen made the crucial change when they brought on Rob McDonald for Ron Jans. Hull-born attacking midfielder McDonald had carved out a seven-year career in the Netherlands. He played for Willem II, scoring 17 league goals in 33 games in 1981/82. In 86 appearances for Groningen over three seasons, he scored 41 league goals before moving to PSV Eindhoven, and in 24 league games he netted 15 goals. You could tell from the technique, calmness and style of how he finished that he knew the way to goal.

When a free kick was awarded in the 68th minute, it struck the wall but squeezed through, falling nicely to McDonald who reacted first to turn in a great left-footed shot for the winner. Feyenoord's winning run was over and 17,000 fans in the Stadion Oosterpark went wild.

Was this time for the team to sit down, re-think and re-calibrate? Perhaps they were too over-confident after thumping Haarlem. The caravan had a flat tyre, but the league campaign would roll on. Significantly, the one game Cruyff missed through injury, Feyenoord lost.

Chapter 15

Total Football and Mind-set

WHEN DISCUSSING Cruyff we are duty-bound to consider the origins of Total Football. Prepare to be surprised. While Rinus Michels was pivotal in spreading the word of Total Football with Cruyff the embodiment of it, the concept had been around for decades before that.

If Rinus Michels was God, then Cruyff was his disciple and the message was Total Football. They initially worked on the project when they teamed up at Ajax but it was not complete until Cruyff and his wonderful Dutch side headed to the World Cup in West Germany in 1974. Journalists christened this style of play Total Football and it is often attributed to this wonderful side but this is when the term was coined. Cruyff and his team-mates stylised the concept and the Netherlands put the theory of playing this way on the map, but they were far from its creators.

Cruyff was someone who wanted to spread the word of this beautiful way of playing. When broken down, Total Football is a style of play which expects that every player can play anywhere on the park. It is far more complex and complicated than that, but at its most basic, this is what is required. But where did it come from? Who devised it?

This style of play, it could be argued, had its roots in the Austrian national team of 1930. Manager Hugo Meisl had been influenced by Jimmy Hogan, one of the early pioneers of the game on mainland Europe. Hogan was one of the continent's first real innovators. England-born and of Irish descent, he had a modest career for Burnley, Fulham and Bolton. Like many of his ilk, though, he excelled in coaching. He started at Dordrecht in the Netherlands before taking over the national side. He then moved to Hungary and Germany. His secret was simple: he made players work more with the ball in training. More practice, more games; even if they were running and working on stamina, they would do drills involving the ball. He was a keen fan of the quick passing style adopted by Scottish side Queen's Park, which was unusual at the time with the preferred tactical approach more a long ball cavalry charge. Hogan's teams played with wing-backs and attacking centre-backs but pushed and passed. Austria are widely regarded as the first national side to embrace and implement what would, through the decades, evolve into Total Football in 1974.

Football historians argue the River Plate side of the 1940s could lay claim to the 'new' system popularised by the Dutch. Rinus Michels has stated he loved watching the Argentine superstar Adolfo Pedernera play. 'The Maestro' was one of the best players in the world during this era and Michels was inspired to try a similar approach and setup. Then in the 1950s, the Hungarian team featuring Puskás continued with this

Total Football style, dominating football and revolutionising the game.

Meanwhile, at Ajax English coaches Jack Reynolds and Vic Buckingham adopted and developed a method of play which would eventually filter down to Michels and Cruyff before reaching Stefan Kovács. Kovács himself lays claim to be one of the most overlooked football coaches of all time. He was their quiet man, their Bob Paisley to Michels's Shankly. Kovács coached Ajax to back-to-back European Cup victories.

Ernst Happel, an Austrian player then manager in the 1960s and 1970s, and a keen student of the Austrian style of play, brought Total Football to Feyenoord and used it effectively to win the 1970 European Cup Final in Milan. He would manage the Netherlands in the 1978 World Cup, taking them to the final.

It was a style of football fuelled by fluidity and use of space, and it required great stamina and fitness, which suited Michels perfectly. He was a fitness fanatic, obsessed with work rate and discipline. Relentless energy and effort is required when players have to press and swamp the opponent. This makes the pitch big. Total Football also involves playing with a high defensive line.

Cruyff's approach to Total Football was simple. For him, the system was only as good as the type of person playing it. Your team-mates had to be disciplined, prepared to work and be unselfish. If they didn't show any of these qualities, it didn't work. Cruyff was blunt about it, 'Total Football requires talented footballers acting in a disciplined group. Someone who whines or doesn't pay attention is a hindrance to the rest.' Cruyff spent years explaining the concept but Total Football is mostly based around distance and positioning, 'When you have the distances and the formation right, everything falls into place.'

In his autobiography, Cruyff gives a practical example of the concept with a real move situation, 'When putting pressure on a right-footed defender, I would close him down on his right, forcing him to pass with his weaker left foot. Meanwhile, Johan Neeskens would be coming up from the midfield on his left, forcing the opponent to make a pass quickly … to do that, Neeskens had to let his man go. That meant his opponent was unmarked but the guy couldn't track Neeskens because, from our defence, Wim Suurbier had pushed up to fill Neeskens's position.' Suurbier was regarded as one of the first modern defenders who would play as a wing-back and attack too. Players like Arie Haan were pivotal to the success of Total Football.

Often unnoticed but critical to the Ajax take on Total Football, Michels brought in tough Yugoslav defender Velibor Vasović from Partizan Belgrade. Straight out of central casting, even his name sounds like a Bond baddie. You know when anyone described as 'Yugoslav defender Velibor Vasović' checks through customs at Schiphol, he is not coming to Amsterdam to sell flowers down by the canal.

When Vasović came in, he turned things around and fitted in perfectly. He also understood his role. 'I played the last man in defence, the libero,' explained Vasović. 'Michels made this plan to play very offensive football. We discussed it. I was the architect, together with Michels, of the aggressive way of defending.' The sweeper would provide the steel and the foundations that would allow his team-mates to apply the grace notes and silk. Ajax won four league titles between 1966 and 1970, and in 1969 they lost the European Cup Final to AC Milan.

Michels marshalled and organised. Vasović showed the kids being promoted from the youth side how to play on the edge and how to play a more ruthless, professional style of football. They needed to toughen up and play to win. Maybe because he came in with a fresh eye, he hadn't been influenced by the systems set in play through the youth structure at the club. Vasović defended, Neeskens aggressively pressed, hunting down the opposition's playmaker. When they used the space, a high defensive line meant the opposition's chances to play were limited. The side were drilled and trained until they reached a point when they instinctively knew their part in the process.

Ajax legend Sjaak Swart, a forward who in this system interchanged to defence and who played for the club from 1956 to 1973, scoring 170 league goals in 170 appearances, explained, 'When I saw Wim Suurbier going forward, I knew I had to go back, I didn't have to be told. And after two years everybody knew what to do.'

When trying to work out how Ajax played, it's easiest to think of a system with a 4-3-3 and defenders who can play in attack. Imagine the full length of a park split into three equal vertical zones. On the left, you had Krol, Mühren and Keizer. In the central zone, you had Vasović, Neeskens and Cruyff and on the right, Suurbier, Haan and Swart, each player switching and interchanging. They had played together over such an extended period, it became second nature.

You had the footballing eloquence and intelligence of Cruyff, who was able to influence and control, then sometimes change the shape of a game tactically during matches without looking to his coach on the bench for help. For Cruyff, it was about tactics, 'With most players, tactics are missing. You can divide tactics into insight, trust and daring. In the tactical area, I think I have more than most other players.' Michels allowed Cruyff to maraud and look for weaknesses to craft an opening in the opposition. He was allowed to track back, play through the middle but would also fall back into central midfield and orchestrate and dictate the shape of the game when he felt he had to. As well as shape and thought, there was brawn and hard work too. There was the relentless hounding down with the high press of Neeskens, forcing opponents deep into their half.

The approach started to pay off as Ajax won more and more games, eventually winning the league. The original model started as 4-2-4 but morphed into a 4-3-3. So, in the mid-1960s, Michels set in place a benchmark that would remain a major part of Dutch football culture and become a style the Netherlands would play, most famously on their way to the 1974 World Cup Final in West Germany. Cruyff would apply his favoured system, over-ruling his coach, in 1983/84 at Feyenoord.

When Cruyff began coaching at Barcelona, he got the team to play in this style. The next generation of Dutch players, like Rijkaard, Gullit and van Basten, then later Dennis Bergkamp, would spread the word. One of Cruyff's prodigies from Barcelona, Pep Guardiola, would use this style effectively and successfully when he was at Barcelona, Bayern Munich and then Manchester City as coach.

Ajax would fall back into a lull for a while but in the last ten years they have started to return to the values of Total Football laid down by Michels and Cruyff and are playing again in the tradition of the club. Under the same methods Cruyff set in play, focusing on technique, and bringing young players through from the academy, Ajax returned to their business model, achieving great results in the Champions League while selling their homegrown talent for a huge profit. Arsene Wenger, while Arsenal manager, was also influenced by this approach and loved attacking, entertaining football. The Dutch and especially the Spanish international sides would use Total Football to great effect.

Not only did Cruyff popularise the format of Total Football, he made another lasting development in the modern game with the necessity of having a goalkeeper unafraid to come off his line and play as a sweeper. At Bayern Munich, Guardiola had Manuel Neuer and at Manchester City he signed Ederson. Before Ederson moved to the Etihad, they leaked like a local church roof shorn of its lead. Guardiola wanted the keeper, who early in his career played at left-back. He had the vision and skill to play, if not the energy. Ederson modestly told Sky Sports, 'When I started playing football, I played in defence as a left-back, but given that I was too lazy to run after the opposition's attacking players I asked the coach to put me in goal and that's how my passion for the position was born.' So Pep had competent footballers playing in goal who loved to play it out from the back.

After the Dutch had beaten Brazil to reach the World Cup Final in 1974, journalist Hugh McIlvanney attempted to work out what he had witnessed. He cast a cold, tactical eye over proceedings and would describe it thus, 'The swirl of movement this involvement produces often makes it difficult to discern a pattern, largely because their patterns are usually organic and spontaneous, rather than preconceived. They can be extremely hard and when they lose the ball they harry and pressurise to get it back. Perfumo, the vastly experienced Argentine defender, whose already miserable World Cup was made worse by the Dutch, recalls an example. "I received the ball from a short free kick, and I looked up and seven Holland players were running at me, it was unnerving."'

The Dutch style of play had captured the imagination of football fans throughout the world. After they had beaten Brazil, football fans wanted to know the secret of their system. Arie Haan, the Dutch midfielder who switched back to play as a sweeper, was explicit and forthcoming about what was being called 'Total Football', whether he liked it or not: 'People talk of Total Football as if it is a system, something to replace 4-2-4 or 4-3-3. It is not a system.' He continued, appearing slightly irritated at those listening who failed to grasp his point, 'As it is at any moment, so you play. That is how we understand it. Not one or two players make a situation but five or six. The best is that with every situation, all 11 players are involved but this is difficult. In many teams maybe only two or three play and the rest are looking. In this team, if you are 60 metres from the ball, you are playing.'

It should be highlighted that Austria's Wunderteam, Hungary's Magical Magyars, and the Netherlands' gloriously sumptuous and effortlessly stylish side of 1974, despite being lauded for Total Football and their style of play, won hearts but failed to win the World Cup. Perhaps any side wanting to play football the correct way should consider the most crucial component of the game, to win. By the time the Dutch side reached the finals in West Germany, they were organised and primed. Their stylish way of playing was lauded because it was the antithesis of the kick and rush of the English, or the anti-football catenaccio of the Italians.

Cruyff may have been one of the greatest footballers ever, but his dedication and desire to play Total Football wound people up. His belief in Total Football being the only way would drive others crazy. He had that uncompromising mentality that only elite level athletes have. He possessed a mindset that believes there are two ways of doing it, my way or the wrong way. Dennis Bergkamp thought it was part of his nature, 'He is very instinctive. He really sees a lot of things, and yes, he's got a dominating character as well, an urge to control things. But that's Total Football, you want to see everything. If you are a total footballer, you can't just be doing your own thing. You have to have the whole picture on the pitch and outside as well.'

Sometimes in football, players, coaches and directors buy into that and when they agree, you have harmony and a collective ethos throughout a club. Equally, it can go desperately wrong, especially when executives, administrators and players or coaches have an almighty clash. When that time comes, it can become dramatic. The player or manager is first to go. The owner, chairman, or president somehow seems to hold on.

Pelé and Cruyff believed football should be played the correct way. It was the beautiful game, after all. They also believed they had to win in the correct way: the key was to play it beautifully and win the game. Another favourite adage of Cruyff's, 'Quality without results is pointless, results without quality is boring,' backs this up. This singular mindset meant Cruyff was also an antagonistic control freak. He was ruthless. Total Football required a concerted team effort, it was demanding and the bar was set high.

A look back at his career clearly shows someone fond of starting an argument, sometimes when it suited him to deliberately engineer a situation to fall out with a belligerent director or an irritating and annoying president. Cruyff's perspective, though, would've been that he was doing it for everyone's benefit. He was the artist, the philosopher, the great thinker; they were the non-believers. Their reluctance to follow his methods and their soullessness was a threat to the game, their lack of vision and in Cruyff's head at least, willingness to accept the ordinary, made them the enemy. Cruyff saw himself as an apostle, spreading the word of Total Football. Directors and administrators and club presidents were the infidels. He was the protector of the beautiful game.

Cruyff's favourite Total Football moment occurred in that 1974 clash against Brazil. The *Observer*'s Hugh McIlvanney summed up the player's elegance and the ferocious nature of football perfectly, 'That he is equally happy to arm team-mates or do the killing himself was perfectly demonstrated by his side's two goals on Wednesday. All Brazil's venom could not save them against the skills implicit in those blows.' He noticed Brazil had started to become weary, 'But from the interval onwards, there was only once conceivable result, and by the end, few Brazilian reputations had been salvaged from the wreckage of their World Cup challenge.'

Chapter 16

Season: 1983/84
UEFA Cup, St Mirren, Spurs, Hoddle and Hooliganism

LEADING INTO the first De Klassieker of the season, Feyenoord had travelled to Scotland to face St Mirren in the UEFA Cup. Cruyff would later grow to love Scotland because of the golf courses, particularly the Old Course at St Andrews which was, conveniently enough, a regular place Barcelona would use for their pre-season preparations. Dundee United happened to train at St Andrews University. While Barca trained at St Andrews and played friendlies against east coast sides like Dundee United and Hibernian, Cruyff would be out on the golf course.

There was no time to play a round on this occasion as they flew over on 14 September 1983 to play a fine St Mirren side at their old ground, Love Street. A crowd of 10,211 packed in to see the hosts valiantly take on the Dutch giants. The Scots were unlucky. They had been moulded into an effective and powerful team, coached by Ricky McFarlane, and should've got more from the match. John 'Cowboy' McCormack valiantly man-marked Cruyff but the star of the show was Ruud Gullit, the man of the match, who scored the only goal of the night after 29 minutes.

Sadly, this game would be marred by the racist abuse aimed at Gullit. If those shouting at the player want to understand the long-term effect of racial abuse and spitting on people because of their colour, listen to Gullit. You can hear the deep emotional scarring it has left. Gullit was a few years into his stellar career in 1983, one which would see him play for Feyenoord, PSV Eindhoven, AC Milan, Sampdoria and Chelsea and appear in some of central Europe's more right-wing nations for club and country. Many of those were hardly places renowned for their tolerance and open-mindedness yet it's a game against St Mirren, in Paisley, Scotland, which still troubles him to this day. Gullit, decades later, said, 'The Scots booed me because of my colour. It started at the warm-up and went on when I scored. I was even spat on. It was the saddest night of my life in football.'

Not everyone in Paisley or Scotland is the same. We apologise for that, we'd like to think we have learned from this time and as always, some idiots ruin it for everyone. Though in 2014, after signing for £2.4m from Groningen, Celtic's Virgil van Dijk was subjected to 'monkey chants and ape-like gestures' from a St Mirren fan. It's about actions, and how we are perceived. It's not only St Mirren and Scottish football, indeed Scottish society has a problem. Scotland loves to imagine itself as a warm, welcoming, open-minded and tolerant country, but we are not. It is delusional to assume we are. Things are improving but racism and homophobia still exist, not only in the working-class backwaters but across many facets of society.

Cruyff would play in Scotland four times in competitive games across his career. In 1970/71, he played for Ajax against Celtic in the European Cup. The quarter-final second leg was at Hampden, in front of 83,000 fans. Celtic were down 3-0 from the first leg, and, despite winning 1-0, they went out. Cruyff's side would go on to win the trophy for the next three years.

In 1973, he played against Rangers in the first leg at Ibrox in the inaugural European Super Cup, when the winners of the European Cup faced the victors of the Cup Winners' Cup. (UEFA refused to sanction it as the official first game of the competition because Rangers were still serving a ban from a pitch invasion at the Nou Camp). Ajax won 3-1, with Cruyff laying on Johnny Rep for the first goal. He scored the second when he turned inside to guide a great left-footed shot past McCloy in the Rangers goal. Arie Haan made it three for Ajax, in front of a 58,000 crowd.

The third occasion was his imperious performance against Celtic in 1982, a 2-2 draw, during his second spell at Ajax. Then there was the appearance with Gullit in the UEFA Cup at Love Street. Feyenoord would have been confident with an away goal to take into the second leg. But St Mirren wouldn't roll over and Feyenoord had to remain focused to make sure they got through.

For the return on 28 September, a side containing future Scotland coach Stevie Clarke and names like Frank McAvennie, Billy Stark and Tony Fitzpatrick were eventually beaten 2-0. The first goal, fit to win any game, came from Wim van Til, a spectacular shot from a wide angle. The ball came from a corner, bounced high out of the box and fell to van Til who met it perfectly, firing it into the top corner. The second came after pressure from Feyenoord when the ball fell to Andrey Zhelyaskov in the six-yard box. St Mirren left Rotterdam with their pride intact, having fought hard against tough opposition and two of the finest Dutch players ever to play the game, Cruyff superbly rounding off and Gullit beginning what would be an extraordinary career.

Throughout his time in the game, Cruyff had strong links with Scotland. In one of the more bizarre stories, it transpired that in 1980 the manager of the struggling First Division side Dumbarton, Sean Fallon, made an audacious approach to Cruyff to bring him to Boghead. The story stuck – because it was true. Even the *Glasgow Herald* led with 'Cruyff Is the Target of Dumbarton Bid', so it must have been correct. Around this point, Fallon spoke to him and hoped, with gates trebling, that the club would be able to lure and pay the superstar. Fallon confirmed the outrageous bid before his death in 2013, 'I knew it was always unlikely we would get Cruyff, but the way I saw it, we couldn't lose. Cruyff was struggling a bit financially in those days because he'd lost all his money in a bad investment, so we felt offering him a few thousand pounds per game might tempt him.'

Fallon revealed all in great detail after speaking to Cruyff, commenting on his politeness and how he was knowledgeable about the whole Scottish scene, 'At worst, it got Dumbarton on the back pages for a few days and boosted the club's image and profile, which was very low at that time.'

On a golf trip to Scotland in 2012, Cruyff confirmed the approach but claimed, with more than a glint in his eye, that the Boghead deal broke down as by that age, his muscles needed the sun to recover (thus spoke the man who moved back to play in Amsterdam and worse still, the freezing chill of Rotterdam, hardly hotbeds of blazing muscle revitalising heat). Unfortunately for Dumbarton and Scotland, after leaving LA Aztecs, Cruyff was a free agent and a gun for hire but would end up signing for the Washington Diplomats and the Dumbarton dream would be over.

In the end, as is often the case with these stories, it's the genuine fans who tend to have the best take on the strangeness surrounding unfolding events. One card on the Dumbarton fan site known by the name 'SPL Sub', came off the bench to score the winner when summing it up perfectly, 'Of course, the deal fell through, as the Dutch maestro was not assured of an automatic start, such was Graham Fyfe's form at that time.'

In the UEFA Cup second round, Feyenoord returned to the British Isles, this time to face a strong Tottenham Hotspur side, with a trip to White Hart Lane. In the elegant and stylish Glenn Hoddle, Spurs had one of the best and most cultured footballers in European football. He was the closest that the English game had to Cruyff. A few weeks before this tie, against Watford, he scored one of his most famous goals, one very similar to Cruyff's style. He took the ball, turned the defender and when everyone was expecting the powerful low shot to the left or right, Hoddle audaciously chipped the keeper. Spurs were struggling at this point and Hoddle had been dropped but he turned things around with some amazing football.

On the night, Steve Archibald and Tony Galvin both scored twice for Spurs and it was 4-0 by 39 minutes. Tie over and Hoddle was the star. He had a hand in each of the four goals. The first came after he sliced open the Feyenoord defence with a wonderful pass to Hughton whose cross was met by Archibald. The second was created by Hoddle after he played a delightful one-two with Archibald before whipping in a cross for Galvin to head home. Hoddle began the move for the third with a lovely left-footed pass to Falco whose shot was saved, but the ball fell to Mabbutt who stretched and cut it back for Archibald to tap in. The fourth saw Hoddle play a 40-yard pass to Galvin, who obliged, running on to meet it. Hoddle had certainly out-shone Cruyff.

In the second half, Feyenoord came back into the game when Cruyff scored in the 75th minute; Wijnstekers played Cruyff in who shared a one-two with Henk Duut, cut across Gary Stevens and pulled one back. Spurs got slack, defended poorly, and Pierre Vermeulen swung in a corner for Ivan Neilsen to drive a second home six minutes later. Suddenly a tie which looked over was brought back to life again.

The two late away goals gave the game some oxygen and made the second leg at De Kuip an open affair. Feyenoord knew they had to go for it to save the second-round match. The second leg attracted 54,600, hoping their side could pull the tie back.

In the end, the major talking point wasn't Spurs' 2-0 victory with goals in each half from Hughton and Galvin. The game was overshadowed by violence, hooliganism and fighting in the crowd. Sadly, in the 1980s, European football was plagued with this type of behaviour. Spurs went on to meet Bayern Munich in the third round.

Cruyff would later admit he made an error at White Hart Lane in the first leg, 'I wanted to test myself against the young star of the present. Glenn was a great player in my book. He played football the way I wanted to see it played. It was a bad error of judgement by me. I thought I could mark him and keep him quiet. The result shows that I could not. It was only on the pitch I realised how good he really was. I was a shadow without any presence.' Generous praise indeed.

Spurs would eventually go on to win the competition by beating Anderlecht in the final. The Belgian team qualified in controversial circumstances. History has revealed that the 1983 UEFA Cup Final should have been contested between Nottingham Forest and Spurs. Down 2-0 in the first leg of the semi-final, Anderlecht won the return 3-0. Forest had a last-minute legitimate goal disallowed and Anderlecht scored after a very questionable penalty award. Any football fan can accept referees sometimes having a bad game and move on. However, 13 years later in 1997, it was revealed that Anderlecht's chairman had paid the referee a bribe of £27,000 to ensure his team's progress.

In the end, for Cruyff, the UEFA Cup would be beyond Feyenoord and him as a player.

A moment perhaps to ponder and a realisation that the next crop of great players, like Hoddle, were coming through. The competition and both ties against St Mirren and Spurs would be underpinned with two horrific issues in football around 1983/84: racism and hooliganism.

Chapter 17

What Makes an Icon?

IN A world where many talented saxophonists exist, what makes a talented musician remain so when another transcends their field and becomes John Coltrane? With significantly outrageous talent comes a higher level of influence, an artist who thinks differently, who is idiosyncratic.

The iconic legend Coltrane took jazz into another sphere of freedom and expression, with his thought process and approach. In 2018, an album previously thought to be lost, *Both Directions at Once*, was released. Coltrane wasn't being poetic; this was a line he gave to fellow musicians for instruction. He told fellow players to think about starting a sentence in the middle, and then going to the beginning and the end of it at the same time.

As well as becoming a football superstar, Cruyff was also a cultural phenomenon. The era, one of optimism, self-expression and self-belief, seemed perfect for Cruyff. His play, presence and style reflected a brighter future, especially for an emerging Ajax side setting out on a wonderful football odyssey. When he's discussed, he is often compared to John Lennon. However, if people want to compare him to a musician the more accurate choice would be John Coltrane. The idea is not as ridiculous as it first sounds.

Coltrane thought about his art on a different plane. For him, music was about fluidity and thinking differently. It was an existential experience. Cruyff considered football like a mathematical equation, one of patterns, shapes, angles and space. Coltrane famously compared jazz to mathematics and devised the 'Coltrane circle' which is as synonymous with the jazz legend as Total Football is with Cruyff.

In Coltrane's case, he took a recognised system, and updated the circle of fifths, adding his innovations, and called it the 'Coltrane circle'. Cruyff also took an existing template, added his innovations and further popularised the sport with Total Football. He passed it on and now it is played by top sides around the world.

When Cruyff died aged 68 in Barcelona, succumbing to lung cancer in March 2016, we lost not only a great footballer but one of the best the world has ever seen. We also lost someone who transcended his sport, a cultural icon who not only towered above his field but helped redefine it.

How people become iconic is an interesting subject. Why, out of the millions of actors, did Hollywood and the world fall for Marilyn Monroe? Her imperfection made her perfect. She was loved because of her sex appeal, yet there's this astonishingly endearing vulnerability. Titans of stage and screen do not become iconic superstars simply because of their talent. Of all the artists that have existed, why would Picasso be considered iconic? Why would artists like Botticelli, Francis Bacon and Gerrit Dou remain lauded but not iconic?

Perhaps it's a 20th-century construct? Have we created Andy Warhol, Martin Luther King and Charlie Chaplin? What makes the Beatles iconic when artists like the Kinks and the Byrds delivered equally incredible levels of consistent music but remain well respected, hugely loved but not iconic? Why does a truck driver from Tupelo called Elvis Presley become a brand as big as McDonald's or Coca-Cola and an iconic figure? These icons were not perfectly rounded individuals; some had their demons, others were political and had something to say but were flawed.

It wasn't a great time to be a cultural icon in 2016. Not only did we lose Cruyff, David Bowie and Muhammad Ali, but also Prince, Fidel Castro and George Michael. Bowie, arguably, was one of the most influential artists of his generation. What made Prince and Bowie stand out? They had talent and a work ethic, and they refused to rest on their laurels. Neither were perfect but spent a career trying to attain perfection. So did Cruyff.

Muhammad Ali was a sporting icon because of his looks, incredibly quick hands and feet, but he was political, he spoke out, and wasn't called the Louisville Lip for services to lip salve. He knew how to hype up a fight and play the game. He had an opinion. He showed great bravery inside the ring and out. He also knew how to annoy and irritate people.

Icons have to break boundaries. Bowie did. He was one of the most influential musicians of the last 50 years, forever changing and reinventing himself. The question is why or how did Cruyff become iconic? It could be his land of birth. The Netherlands is delightfully off-centre, eccentric and creative; it is only fitting Johan Cruyff came from there.

Perhaps it was the era. The timing was perfect for a creative cultural icon to grow and evolve. Cruyff had the freedom to express himself on and off the park, across three decades. He was 17 in 1964, 27 in 1974 and 37 in 1984, and looked cool wherever he played. He looked equally iconic not only in his Ajax or Dutch national strip but an LA Aztecs kit, even sporting Feyenoord's yellow away shirt. Iconic and legendary status comes to sporting superstars not only through their ability but influence, passion, consistency and charisma.

This was more than a footballer. Cruyff was someone cultural and political – this mattered. Of course, not every footballer can afford to be so outspoken, not financially, but by sheer dint of their talent. Ali and Cruyff could afford to shoot from the hip and lip. It's easy to be opinionated and irritate if you are outrageously brilliant at your day job. Both attained greatness and changed their sport. Some iconic figures transcend their field, do something unique, maybe even have something named after them. I can only think of two footballers with moves or techniques named after them: the 'Cruyff Turn' and 'doing a Panenka' – a technique describing a chipped penalty.

Antonín Panenka himself is deserving, to be remembered at least, for his iconic sporting moment. In the final of the 1976 European Championships, playing for Czechoslovakia against West Germany, the midfielder, a great passer of the ball and something of a dead ball expert with a great right-footed shot, was left to take the deciding penalty in a shootout. If he scored, his country would win the title. Panenka chose to bravely take his penalty in a way which put him in the history books forever.

Until then, penalty takers would run up and wallop it hard into the corner. Panenka's secret, apart from the delicate dink and chip through the centre, worked on many levels. His approach and run-up looked like he planned to thud it high and hard into the corner. He also seemed to run for 12 yards before striking the ball. The goalkeeper has to be convinced the kick will be full of power with intent, and if they are decent, they will dive, but make sure their legs will stay straight if the ball goes down the middle. There's a chance they might still save it. The second part of the skill is to hit the ball lightly and high enough to avoid the keeper's legs and feet. So a powerful shot down the middle would be saved but a slower chip wouldn't.

Panenka explained, 'It's always been a fight between shooter and keeper – who can keep his nerve the longest? No keeper will stay in the centre – that's what I based my strategy on.' When Panenka took this penalty it was a huge moment in world football and the goal which won his nation the trophy. The penalty strike portrayed him as some kind of maverick.

Like most idiosyncratic players, Panenka made it look off the cuff, but their methods are down to practice and work on the training ground. Once he took the penalty, his life changed as he was forever associated with the technique named after him. If you are ever in Prague and want to have a memorable evening, don't say cheers, say 'Panenka'. You'll be lucky to make it home.

Transcending your sport brings incredible power and influence. Cruyff was 36, he still had a season in him, he knew his body better than those at Ajax who wouldn't renew his contract, and he was in great shape. Iconic sportsmen feed off adversity. Ajax had just handed him the motivation he required.

How could they do this to him? He was Joppie, the happy kid from Betondorp, the vegetable delivery boy for this club. He had given far more than any of the directors in front of him ever had. He had cleaned boots and swept floors for this club.

When Cruyff decided to join Feyenoord, his nature, psychology, and mentality would kick in. It was time to think of the legendary icon, the Number 14, Cruyff the brand. He would prove them wrong by channelling his aggression with the mentality which made a global footballing superstar. Instead of taking the easy way out, he displayed the attributes of most iconic sportsmen – a belligerent and bloody-minded determination – and would not go out with a whimper.

Contrast him with Pelé, for instance. Despite his wondrous ability on the pitch, something was lacking in the Brazilian's personality. Imagine if he was more outspoken, more controversial instead of so neutral. If he'd had a strong opinion and was more political, like Sócrates, and used his fame and profile to stand up for a cause and used his influence, he would perhaps have been so much more appealing. If Pelé was more flawed, he could have risen to the heights of Che Guevara.

With modern social media outlets, today's stars have incredible reach and influence. Perhaps they are content to be model professionals. The game has changed so much now, and players themselves behave like CEOs of a multinational company. Messi and Ronaldo have been surprisingly impartial when they could have used their fame and influence. I appreciate these debates are always generational. Messi and Ronaldo would need to have a word with their agents, lawyers, representatives, their sponsors, and their PR firms first. They would have to clear any thoughts in case they annoyed any of Messi's 157 million Instagram and 3 million Twitter followers. Incidentally, Ronaldo has 227 million Instagram pals and 85.9 million followers on Twitter.

Yet here are two players from working-class backgrounds, who, along with their families, sacrificed so much to reach extraordinary heights and find success. They would be wonderful role models and people would flock to them if they were political and outspoken on something, say, like the environment. Maybe they are both so highly focused as modern professionals and are advised, for their endorsements and commercial deals, to remain neutral. However great they are, and what an incredible haul of goals, awards and plaudits have come their way, they are not iconic. They are great. But to be iconic, I believe you need to be flawed.

You could only wonder what Cruyff would be like on social media if he was a contemporary now with access to the same high-profile social media outlets. Despite what his sponsors or management team told him, he would be irate at Brexit, the way Covid-19 was handled and racism across Europe and currently in 2020, especially in America. Cruyff stood out in his era because he could deliver football on the park and deliver a great line off it. He knew his opinion carried weight, as did Sócrates.

When discussing the best ever footballers, people often compare goals scored, caps gained and trophies won. Then it would be Messi and Ronaldo, hands down. But Cruyff and Maradona did it when there was less money, the pitches were worse and in teams which were not always brimming with talent. Maradona's game and his build made him more subject to savage brutality. He was continually chopped down by opponents. If you're doing any comparisons and making lists by medals and trophies and goals, you are missing the point of football.

I would want to see players like Sócrates, with his languid style and intelligence, recognised. Perhaps Zinedine Zidane, too, who has come closest to hitting the upper echelon by scoring great goals in top games and winning the World Cup and of course, is flawed. With Maradona, there was an incredible ability to rip through opponents and win games on his own, though if both those men played today, they'd struggle to fit into systems and the discipline of a high pressing game.

I know it's generational and I used to get bored when I heard older guys talking about Di Stéfano and Puskás and then it was Eusébio and Pelé, Beckenbauer and Cruyff. Both Messi and Ronaldo are exceptional footballers but what separates them from greatness is their robotic perfection. What made Cruyff, Maradona, Best and even Puskás iconic was their beautiful imperfection.

Save for the odd blind spot for their taxes, Messi and Ronaldo are not flawed enough to be icons. Johan Cruyff annoyed people, particularly journalists. He was named European Footballer of the Year in 1971 and 1973, at a time he was also winning three successive European Cups. It's not too shabby. It makes you wonder how outstanding you needed to have been in 1972 to have won the Ballon d'Or.

Instead, UEFA member countries awarded their prize for the best player in Europe to the West German superstar Franz Beckenbauer. They are entitled to their opinion; I don't agree with it. Cruyff played one of his best-ever games in the 1972 European Cup Final. Being outspoken can come back to bite you, as demonstrated by Ajax's rejection after everything he'd done for them.

Pelé and Maradona were Cruyff's footballing equals, but neither the Brazilian nor Argentine came close to him in terms of the way he influenced the modern game. If football was a religion, he was the supreme leader. The best. He transformed football, firstly at Ajax, then Barcelona. Cruyff invented modern football.

Perhaps the final word on the debate should go to legendary Argentine coach César Luis Menotti, who has an interesting take on the best ever players, 'There have been four kings of football – Di Stéfano, Pelé, Cruyff and Maradona – and the fifth has not yet appeared. We are awaiting the fifth and it is sure to be Messi but so far he is not among the kings.'

The football world was rocked to its core when Maradona passed away on 25 November 2020. Argentina entered three days of mourning. Maradona's coffin was draped in both an Argentina flag and a Number 10 football shirt, as his body lay in state in the presidential palace for the day. Thousands flocked to say goodbye to the icon. Such was the confusion, grief and fervour of those waiting that police in riot gear, struggled to hold back the crowd and had to close the palace. As his funeral procession was driven through Buenos Aires, flanked by police outriders to Bella Vista cemetery, on the outskirts of the city, the chaos and anguish, interjected with brief seconds of serenity, only mirrored the player's life. They had lost another king. Life was over, aged just 60 for Diego.

Chapter 18

Barca Coaching –
Something in the Air

CRUYFF WENT to Barcelona having impressed at Ajax. He had won the Dutch Cup and the European Cup Winners' Cup, finding new talent like Marco van Basten and Dennis Bergkamp, but was brought in as coach, mainly because of his attacking style of play. It is beyond doubt that during Cruyff's time as Barcelona head coach from 1988 to 1996, which saw him win 11 trophies in eight years, something magical was occurring. Not only did Cruyff bring success, glamour, excitement and entertainment to the Catalan people, playing an attractive brand of football, but his reign was also littered with coincidences, and outrageous reversals and swings in fortune that suggested something miraculous was in the air.

Cruyff's blend of experience, foreign imports and a youth team and reserve side who played the same way, heralded an unprecedented period of success. He won four LaLiga titles in a row from 1990/91 to 1993/94. In 1992, his Dream Team won the club's first European Cup.

Barcelona romped to the title in 1990/91, ten points clear of Atlético Madrid. In 1991/92 for example, Barcelona reached the European Cup Final and faced Sampdoria at Wembley, but they nearly didn't make it. They came close to going out in the second round against German champions FC Kaiserslautern and, after a convincing 2-0 home win in the Nou Camp, headed to Germany confident. However, Kaiserslautern were on fire in the Fritz-Walter-Stadion. They were 3-0 up and on their way to the third round but up popped Barcelona's Bakero to score in the 90th minute. The night finished 3-1 and Barca were through thanks to that away goal.

When they eventually reached the final, the game was a tight, goalless draw and headed into extra time. The breakthrough ultimately came in the 112th minute when Ronald Koeman thundered home a free kick. But FC Kaiserslautern's players and fans, as they watched the game, would be well within their rights to wonder why a team they had beaten 3-1 had won the trophy. Barca's luck would continue.

In the last league game of that season, Barcelona were at home to Athletic Bilbao. They won 2-0 with Hristo Stoichkov scoring in each half. They had done their part but weren't expecting it to turn into such a special day. Before the game, Barcelona had received a guard of honour from their opponents and held the European Cup aloft for their fans to see. It was that kind of day, a celebration of the first European Cup win, but the league was over and they were resigned to finishing second.

The title had been a three-horse race between Barcelona, Real Madrid, and Atlético Madrid. The last-day fixtures heavily favoured Real, who were playing away to Tenerife. No one expected a miracle and Leo Beenhakker's team were two up inside 28 minutes. The first came from a Fernando Hierro header and some poor goalkeeping at the far post after only eight minutes. There was no doubt with the second goal, a brilliant free kick from Gheorghe Hagi. Quique Estebranze pulled one back for Tenerife to make it 2-1 at half-time.

Even the staunchest of Catalans would be lying if they expected anything other than Madrid to rattle in four or five in the second half. But there was magic in the air, remember. The game turned in the 77th minute when Brazilian centre-half Ricardo Rocha scored an own goal. However, a minute later, substitute Pier scored for Tenerife to make it 3-2. The Nou Camp buzzed – fans with radios started to share the news. First, they revealed that Madrid had scored an own goal and it was 2-2. Then, as the noise faded slightly, a second wave quickly spread throughout the cavernous arena. Tenerife had taken the lead. They would hold on until full time to deliver a sensational upset.

Meanwhile, in the Nou Camp, Barca's game had finished and their points were in the bag. The squad and management remained on the pitch, surrounded by press, TV and radio. They would be doing a lap of honour with the European Cup anyway. Camera crews and mics were in Cruyff's face as news of the full-time score came in and sparked glorious celebration. In an astonishing turn of events, Barcelona had been crowned champions. Another unexpected party, an even sweeter one – it was surreal, wonderful and unforgettable. Both teams had won 23 games, with Barcelona pipping their rivals to the title by a point.

Perhaps Cruyff's tenure at Barca was blessed, at least at the start. There was a strange feeling of déjà vu for the culmination of 1992/93. Not only did the league race come down to the final day of the season again, but uncannily it also saw Real Madrid take on Tenerife in the Estadio Heliodoro Rodríguez López.

On the final day, Barcelona trailed Real by a point, and focused on their last home game, this time against Real Zaragoza, more out of hope than expectation. This time the odds were longer, Tenerife couldn't do them a favour again, could they? Madrid would surely lift the title.

The score filtered through from Santa Cruz, where Tenerife had taken the lead after 11 minutes through Oscar Dertycia. Before half-time, Chano doubled their lead. Barcelona scored after 13 minutes through Stoichkov's 20th goal of the season. They did their part of the deal and Tenerife helped them out once again, Cruyff's side once more winning the title by a point in unexpected circumstances on the final day.

Reports later emerged the Real manager had tried to change the routine from the previous year and chartered two smaller planes. One of them had a fault with the air conditioning and temperatures soared on board to 50 degrees; players were ill, dehydrated and it had to return to Madrid. The journey, in the end, took 15 hours, and when you watch the game knowing this, you can see the Madrid players are drained and wilting.

The climax of 1993/94 was similarly bizarre, going to the final game. This year, the challenge was from Real, though not Madrid, but Real Club Deportivo de La Coruña, informally known as Deportivo. Deportivo had captured the hearts of the

Spanish public. The nation appeared captivated by the romance of the provincial side from Galicia, who broke Barcelona and Real Madrid's domination of the league. Real Madrid had what football presidents and pundits euphemistically describe as a season in transition but what football fans call an absolute shocker. They lost 12 games and were even pushed down to fourth place by Real Zaragoza.

Everyone watched Deportivo, who needed a win to clinch LaLiga. It was theirs to lose. Deportivo had been performing brilliantly thanks to their experienced coach, Arsenio Iglesias, the 'Wizard of Arteixio' (Arteixio has some idyllic beaches, beautiful and secluded and reminiscent of Scottish beaches on a remote island inlet). Iglesias was ruthlessly efficient in defending and his goalkeeper Francisco Liaño was in the form of his life, with 26 clean sheets. They also had three high-quality Brazilians in Silva, Bebeto and Donato.

In the last part of the season, Barcelona had started playing like their league campaign was over. They relaxed, performed without tension, and won a run of games, including a crucial match against Deportivo. They were playing fast-flowing and attacking football, winning five matches on the bounce and scoring 22 goals. Romário and Stoichkov were scoring for fun thanks to the creativity of Michael Laudrup. Romário would end the season with 30 goals and win that campaign's Pichichi trophy as the leading scorer. Like an experienced thoroughbred racehorse, Barcelona were coming from behind and exerting pressure while waiting for their moment to pounce.

As Barcelona piled pressure on the leaders, Deportivo started to draw several games but they would respond, proving they had what it took to win the title. They remained resolute, played with belief and stayed on top, winning five games in a row. They went into the last four games three points ahead but then dropped points to two sides who would be relegated. In the penultimate game week, Barca had to face a stabilised, more organised Real Madrid, under the new coach Vicente Del Bosque at the Bernabéu.

Still on top, Deportivo could be forgiven for thinking they might have the league in the bag. Barca hadn't won El Clásico in the Bernabéu for ten years. Real Madrid played well but Barcelona won, with a late Amor goal. Deportivo beat Logroñés and the caravan moved on to the last game.

Both were at home and the nation was watching. Deportivo hosted Valencia and Barcelona faced Sevilla. Both matches would kick off at the same time, and Deportivo had the upper hand in that if they won or matched the Barca result, they would be champions. In the Nou Camp, Sevilla's Simeone opened the scoring before Stoichkov equalised but Davor Šuker scored a second before half-time to take Sevilla 2-1 ahead. It was still goalless at the Riazor in Deportivo's game. As it stood, Deportivo would be crowned champions.

Barcelona came out in the second half and after five minutes, Stoichkov fired in the equaliser. It was tense until the 70th minute when Romário made it 3-2 for Barca. The 'As It Stands' graphic flipped into overdrive and Barcelona had moved into pole position in the title race. Barca, calling on their past experiences, knew what they had to do. They continued to apply more pressure and Laudrup and Bakero made it 5-2. Yet this would all be in vain if Deportivo scored.

The Deportivo fans travelled to the ground hoping for a party but on hearing how things were starting to unfold in Barcelona, their packed stadium remained unnaturally quiet. They were so nervous as they struggled to encourage their side on, and the tension appeared to reach the pitch. Time was surely running out.

Deportivo sensed their chance to beat Barcelona to the crown was gone. Their extraordinary season was petering out. They attacked in waves but nothing went their way. Again, Barcelona had done their part but there was a feeling of resignation among those present. They couldn't be so lucky again, could they? Surely Deportivo would get it done and clinch the title. Barcelona had done their job, and it was a case of waiting. Then a reaction from the fans reached the players, slowly percolating around the stadium. Something had happened. Barca were still in the race.

In the 90th minute, the Barca crowd started to bubble up and react to something. Cruyff was looking around, telling everyone to remain calm. They shrugged shoulders, shook their heads, looked confused and then disappointed. Deportivo must have got their goal. No, not quite. Instead, they had been awarded a penalty, in the last minute.

The Deportivo crowd reached fever pitch. In Barcelona, there was disbelief. A penalty to Deportivo? In the 90th minute? The tension was unbearable. The trouble was that Deportivo's normal penalty taker, Bebeto, had missed a few and had been taken off duties. Donato was now the man with the task but he was off the pitch. The responsibility fell to defender Miroslav Đukić. He looked nervous before he took it and no wonder, with such a responsibility on his shoulders.

The Deportivo fans did not help the situation as they were practically celebrating the title win when the penalty was awarded. In Barcelona, the fans were ruefully accepting that the league was over. Virtually the entire campaign was over and the destination of the title hinged on this penalty. Unbelievably, Valencia's González Vázquez saved it. There was despair at Deportivo's Riazor and ecstasy at the Nou Camp. Fans nervously listened to their radios, waiting on the full-time whistle, on the last minute of the last game on the final day of the season. Barca had won their fourth title in a row.

Over the years, we've had many last-minute goals deciding titles. But rarely has a title been won by one kick of the ball. Miroslav Đukić showed amazing strength of character to step up and take that penalty. But imagine having to live with that for the rest of your life?

Something special was definitely in the air.

Chapter 19

Season 1983/84:
The KNVB Cup Run

THIS 1983/84 season would see Feyenoord not only win the league but emerge as winners of the Dutch Cup. The Dutch national cup competition, the KNVB Beker, is still highly regarded and much coveted. It is one of the few domestic cup competitions in Europe still taken seriously. Clubs field full-strength sides and play to win. In the 1983/84 season, the winners gained automatic entry into the European Cup Winners' Cup. Today, they secure entry into the Europa League.

For sides across Europe, the league title is the Holy Grail and due to the increased revenue generated via qualification for the Champions League, the cups have often been sacrificed for the far more lucrative top-four place.

Feyenoord set out on their cup campaign of 1983/84, and with Cruyff in tow would have felt, with a bit of luck, that they could win it. To win your national cup competition is a wonderful achievement and, if you can claim the league, it makes the cup victory twice as sweet. Most double-winning sides become the stuff of legend at clubs. However, to win the double, aged 37, in a major European league, in your last season as a professional, would be a sensational achievement.

A successful cup run galvanises the support. Cruyff was fond of domestic titles and in future years the cup would keep him in a job at Barcelona when he coached his side to a Copa del Rey victory in his second season at the club. In football's modern era, a great cup run is often dismissed, but most fans understand having your team's name on the trophy as that year's cup holders trumps a money-spinning fourth-place finish to qualify for the Champions League.

It's not easy to win a cup. Competitions can be difficult to navigate through and often provide shock results, especially if lower-league sides make it through the qualifying sections with the chance of drawing a big club. There's also something magical when the underdogs welcome a huge club and the stars have to rough it, in a small, dilapidated ground, with fans breathing down their necks and squealing no end of abuse and vitriol into their ears.

For the established sides it can be fraught and full of so many unknowns. Cup football loves the dream of minnows attempting a giant-killing on an uneven surface. Across most associations in Europe, the lower league sides can face a big club from the second or third round onwards. In the Netherlands, big sides are part of the competition from round one, making it far more exciting for the neutral and giving smaller clubs the chance to generate a big cash payday.

The winners of the Dutch Cup generally deserve it, and the journey to the final can be nerve-wracking. In this wonderful run, Feyenoord would even face their rivals Ajax, a game which would go to a replay, then extra time.

First up, though, Feyenoord travelled to the province of Friesland to take on Heerenveen. The name was established in 1551 by three lords as an ideal area for digging up peat, thus – *Heer* for Lord and *veen* which means peat.

Cruyff was on form, taking (and falling) at a corner which set up the goal for Hoekstra. The low, driven shot hit the stanchion and bounced out quickly, and only the scorer's celebration gave any hint a goal had been scored. Cruyff, even on his backside, was able to assist in the goal. He was up for it and in the mood, his repertoire of tricks on show. He was doing his stuff, like taking a free kick and crossing the ball from the left with the outside of his right foot.

In an entertaining game, a tremendous 35-yard shot from Ruud Gullit brought a great save from Heerenveen keeper Ad Raven. Much to the delight of the home crowd, while Cruyff did his usual pointing and coaching from the halfway line, he lost the ball and Heerenveen ran up and scored but the goal was disallowed for some reason. The ground was packed tight and Heerenveen took the game to Feyenoord but the away side did enough in what can best be described as an old-fashioned blood and snotters cup tie.

In the second round, on 29 November, Feyenoord welcomed Utrecht-based amateur side Elinkwijk to De Kuip. It says something about the authenticity and sense of fair play of a country's national football tournament when teams involved from the top to the bottom are incorporated into a competition.

Feyenoord saw them off in a convincing 7-0 victory. I wonder if there was a race at the final whistle to swap shirts with Cruyff? Though I'm not even sure if he played. Details are sketchier than a murder at a cartoon sketch workshop. He wasn't among the scorers, that's for sure. Pierre Vermeulen opened the scoring and Gullit added a hat-trick. There was a Michel van de Korput penalty, and further goals from Andre Stafleu and Andrey Zhelyaskov rounded off the tie.

So, after a lowly amateur side, who would fate decree you meet in the cup? Football seems to have an uncanny knack of drawing out the odd cracker of a tie. Do the KNVB have their version of hot and cold balls? Feyenoord would meet Ajax away from home, meaning a nervous return to the scene of the crime (and 8-2 slaughter) for Cruyff's side. An exciting and tense midweek game under floodlights ended 2-2.

In the 20th minute, Cruyff received the ball on the right from Michel van de Korput. He held on to it, luring and tempting three Ajax players on to him, before cleverly slipping it back to the unmarked van de Korput, where the cross was met with a perfectly timed acrobatic right-foot volley by Houtman from 12 yards out. The visitors were a goal up at half-time.

Cruyff was far more visible than on his last visit to De Meer. He was on the ball more, pivotal to Feyenoord's moves, setting up chances and a real part of the action.

While Olsen attacked for Ajax and was about to cross, fans threw a firework directly at Joop Hiele in the Feyenoord goal. It exploded at his leg and you could see the force of the impact hurt him. He was lucky not to be hit full on. Unbelievably, the referee and players ignored it, and they played on. If it happened in today's game, an ambulance, a surgeon and a priest would be called.

Ajax were awarded a penalty after Olsen was brought down in the box, but Ronald Koeman put the resulting kick wide. Slack play and hesitation from Hoekstra then allowed Rijkaard – who came on in the 39th minute as a sub for Peter Boeve – to score a superb goal when he bulleted in a 30-yard right-footed shot past the helpless Hiele.

Cruyff set in motion the move which eventually led to the second Feyenoord goal. He picked the ball up deep in his own half, in the right-back position, and, far too easily, for someone aged 36, found another gear to leave his opponent behind. Instead of continuing to run with the ball, he ran on to it and his first touch was a pass with the outside of his left foot. This fell to an advancing Hoekstra, who played in Gullit perfectly to finish with a brilliant, low, left-footed shot.

Ajax equalised in the 68th minute after Marco van Basten rose to magnificently head home from an accurately taken Felix Gasselich corner. The game would go back to De Kuip for a replay which Feyenoord would eventually win 2-1 after extra time.

They would face an easier challenge in the quarter-final at home to NEC Nijmegen on 4 March, going on to win 6-1. Feyenoord looked tired and unfocused and allowed NEC to score after some uncharacteristically slack defending from Ivan Nielsen. It was Nielsen who then edged forward, perhaps making amends for his earlier mistake, to provide the ball for the equaliser. He lobbed a high, awkward delivery into the box and with NEC unable to deal with it, Hoekstra was first there with the header to make it 1-1. The second goal came after Gullit and Cruyff applied pressure and stretched the NEC defence. When the ball came back to Cruyff he played in Ben Wijnstekers who scored with a terrific shot from 30 yards to make it 2-1.

Cruyff was third on the scoresheet. When the ball fell to him, he could've been forgiven for thinking he was back in America and taking one of their shootouts. When NEC were hesitant in the build-up, they lost possession and the long pass through from Stafleu was seized upon by Cruyff, who remained cool when one-on-one and deftly flicked the ball up and over the advancing keeper, headed it into his own path then put it away sweetly with his left foot into the empty goal. The sparse crowd cheered loudly when his name was called by the stadium announcer.

For the fourth goal, Cruyff crossed from the left with the outside of his right foot from a free kick, and Gullit rose to thunder a powerful header which the NEC keeper Wim van Cuijk was unable to stop.

After the break, Cruyff played another pass through to Gullit who lost his marker and managed to nick it around the goalkeeper before walking it into the net. Before that, he stopped to play to the gallery and celebrate; the fans loved it but you sensed some of the seasoned pros on the park didn't appreciate it too much. Wijnstekers whipped in a brilliant left-footed cross for the final goal. Gullit's header hit the bar and Hoekstra got the sixth when he was quickest to the ball at the back post.

The quality of opposition might not have been top-drawer but Cruyff's play was fantastic, full of penetrating and improbable passes with the sides of both feet. He played regular long, controlled passes through to Gullit and was continually part of the game. He also should've scored a few more goals but was foiled with one amazing save by van Cuijk.

Feyenoord faced another replay after their semi-final against HFC Haarlem ended in a 1-1 draw. I'm assuming this wasn't a classic and the sportswriters found a great pub somewhere and decided en masse to not bother doing any match reports. Information is scarce. Cruyff didn't play and a low crowd of 14,539 witnessed Gullit open the scoring in the second half, only for Haarlem's Wim Balm to equalise nine minutes later. Michel van de Korput was sent off.

Gullit scored first in the replay, reacting quickest to some shocking defending before rounding the goalkeeper to score from a tight angle. Gullit had a hand in the second Feyenoord goal with some probing wide play, and when the ball fell to Henk Duut he let fly with a perfect low strike from 25 yards out. The goalkeeper would not have stopped it and even in slow motion, it seemed to rocket past him. The speed and ferocity of the shot nearly took the nets too.

For the third, Gullit headed on to Hoekstra who, after some clever work made it to the byline, when the goalkeeper committed, trying to close him down. He played it back across for Gullit to calmly score his second at the near post, into an open goal. Haarlem pulled one back before Feyenoord made it four. At this point lines of communication were broken, it must've been cold and the journalists covering the game presumably headed off for a Dutch Bovril. Cruyff had a quiet game but still managed to show the odd bit of class.

In one move he accelerated and dribbled by three opponents before trying an audacious lob over the goalkeeper from 18 yards out.

Gullit was on a great run of form, and it must have been both amazing and frustrating for Feyenoord fans at the time to witness how brilliant he was. You could see he was destined to become a world-class player. Throughout each game of this season, he shone. He was still raw at times but had that presence and confidence. It would be a frustration, too, because clubs had started to notice and he would soon be off.

The Dutch association usually circulated the final around the country, and as luck would have it, the 1984 final took place on 2 May at Feyenoord's De Kuip. It would provide a match-up between the Rotterdammers and Fortuna Sittard. The game itself was a nervous affair and Cruyff stood out, having some great runs, wonderful crosses and numerous great link-ups with Wijnstekers. Sittard took the game to Feyenoord though, bringing out some superb saves from Joop Hiele.

Gullit had a better second half and as the final started to open up it turned when Houtman came on as a sub in the 69th minute for Willy Carbo. Cruyff, still controlling the game at the age of 37, began the move which led to the only goal. He played a long pass with the outside of his right foot through to Hoekstra, who laid it off for Gullit to play in a perfect, angled cross to Houtman who headed toward the goal – then followed in to make sure. Fortuna Sittard had a great chance to take it to extra time late on, but the shot was driven over the bar. They also came close with a fine free kick, which was again saved by Hiele.

Feyenoord would win the cup and celebrate in front of their fans, who had swapped places. The players received the trophy in the stand and Feyenoord fans applauded from the pitch after a full-scale invasion.

Chapter 20

Núñez v Cruyff

CRUYFF HAD many adversaries but it's fair to say his arch-nemesis was Barcelona's president Josep Lluís Núñez. They didn't get on at all. Interestingly, Núñez was forever at odds with Maradona, too. Perhaps no one was allowed to be bigger than the club, or him? In 1978, as a Barcelona player and having announced he would retire at the end of the season, Cruyff had an acrimonious fall-out with him over a tax bill when the tax rules were changed for Spanish football.

In Spain, for years, clubs had always helped pay the players' taxes. The players negotiated their contracts after tax, based on a net wage. The change to the system meant that players became responsible for paying their own taxes but, to attract the best players, clubs continued to help cover the shortfall. Players found themselves obliged to pay retrospectively so clubs helped pay those debts, at least for those who would still be there the following season. Since Cruyff had already announced he was leaving, Núñez declined to offer any help and Cruyff was forced to meet the tax bill himself. This is exactly the sort of thing Cruyff would have a habit of remembering.

Núñez was a shrewd leader at Barcelona and it may have saved his presidency to reach out in 1988 and approach Cruyff and bring him in as coach, like welcoming back the prodigal son. He would welcome in Lucifer dancing in sequins and a tutu if it guaranteed another term as president.

All coaches, no matter their stature, lose influence and control. Cruyff was no different. He may have coached Barcelona to their first European Cup victory but this was football. Results are everything. Fans grow impatient, and the board become reluctant to provide funding. Players are not blameless here, too. The top ones have an acute sense of self-preservation and will scarper as soon as they sniff their team-mates have lost faith. Coaches are expected to sell their best players, and win with a less talented team. By this point, the board are no longer taking the coach's calls and are unavailable.

Núñez was a successful construction magnate and relished his high-profile role at the Nou Camp. He was very hands-on, would be front and centre whenever the side won a trophy and would be found mixing with the players in the dressing room, celebrating for the cameras and in every photograph for the papers. He loved the role and was often accused by fans of using his position to promote his construction and hotel businesses. When Cruyff returned in 1988 he was blunt to his boss, setting the ground rules from day one. 'If you want to talk to me,' Cruyff told the president, 'I'll come to your office. You don't come to my dressing room.'

Núñez was voted in as president in 1978 and remained in office until 2000. His reign was successful as the club grew under his stewardship and he masterminded an exciting period.

The Nou Camp was expanded to hold 120,000 supporters, a museum and smaller stadium were built, and on Cruyff's suggestion, La Masia (the club's youth academy) was rebooted and restructured, and systems put in place to allow younger players like Andrés Iniesta, Xavi Hernández and Lionel Messi to develop into first-team stars. Núñez was also behind big-name signings like Diego Maradona, Ronaldo, Romário, Michael Laudrup and Hristo Stoichkov.

As Cruyff tried to rebuild, the team finished fourth in 1995 and in his final season they would eventually (though he was sacked before the campaign was completed) finish third. The powerful Catalan media and fans knew he'd been given longer than others would have been. Núñez was used to being the centre of attention so when someone like Cruyff grabbed the spotlight, the atmosphere was difficult and tense. He found the Dutchman's popularity infuriating, so to see him slowly suffer and get his comeuppance was to his taste. He loved success on the park, initially, but Cruyff became bigger than the board and the club. Núñez realised that Cruyff had imparted his personality, philosophy and DNA on the club to the extent he *was* Barcelona. At this point, most football people around the world connected Barca the brand to Cruyff and not Núñez.

By 1994, the cracks started to show in the Cruyff project. Players were leaving and those brought in didn't grasp the urgency or philosophy with enough potency. Núñez knew that deposing Cruyff would require a well-thought-through manoeuvre. Cruyff had become too powerful. The role of president was financial and creative, and he was one for big ideas and sweeping gestures. He had been there before, and, strategically, was clever. Knowing football was a results and performance-driven business, he was aware that if the team didn't win or under-performed then the fans would, however reluctantly, decide Cruyff would need to go.

If the relationship between the two had been more cordial, the president might have taken his coach out for a lavish dinner and convinced him to elect and announce the new coach, move upstairs, become a technical director and remain part of the club's broader goals and aims. But it wasn't.

Núñez understood this was about power, and he approached the situation more like a politician. This would be about the slow dilution of Cruyff's status. He allowed his coach to slowly wither and die on the vine. He exerted pressure on him, as he would be expected to, but the longer Cruyff was allowed to remain, the more he damaged his reputation and legacy.

The club's support and the media had reluctantly forgiven the Dream Team, who as defending champions were defeated by CSKA Moscow in the newly formed Champions League in 1992/93. But if there was a semblance of a working relationship between Cruyff and Núñez, it evaporated in 1994 when Barca were unceremoniously destroyed 4-0 in the Champions League Final by AC Milan.

Cruyff's footballing methods and style of play would be universally lauded, but the way he had set up the team left them open and when they attacked they also conceded goals. When they won the league in 1994, they conceded 42 times. The second-placed side, Deportivo, only let in 28. In their title run-in, Romário and Stoichkov had performed brilliantly for Barcelona and together with Michael Laudrup, their goals tally reached 91 for the season in 38 games. AC Milan scored 36 in 34 in Serie A. Something wasn't right.

Barcelona had won the league on the last day of the season and then played the final in Athens days later. Serie A had been completed two weeks previously. Milan had time to build up towards the final and it paid off with their victory.

From here on in the Dream Team started to disintegrate; the side didn't have the same fervour. After the AC Milan defeat, Cruyff took a gamble and Zubizarreta, Jon Andoni Goikoetxea, Salinas and Laudrup were out. In January, Romário left. When pushed for reasons as to his decision to let the man who scored a hat-trick against Real Madrid go, Cruyff was Cruyff, 'He's not as good as I was. I made others play better; he can only score goals.'

Cruyff's rebuild was taking too long and by 1994/95 Barcelona were in serious decline. They lost ten and drew ten and finished fourth in the table. Núñez continued to allow the slow bloodletting to happen. The worse it got for Cruyff, the more the fans would turn on him, which would make the eventual decision easier and more inevitable. Núñez continued to watch the noose slowly tightening around Cruyff's neck.

In the summer of 1995, Stoichkov, Eusébio, Txiki Begiristain and Ronald Koeman were shown the door and now only four remained: Pep Guardiola, Albert Ferrer, Miguel Angel Nadal and José Marí Bakero. The trouble Cruyff now faced was the lack of dynamism, momentum and impact. Of the new signings – Gheorghe Hagi, Robert Prosinečki, Gică Popescu and Luís Figo – only the latter seemed to grasp the sense of urgency when playing for Barcelona. The turnaround wasn't happening quickly enough. When Núñez's moment came, it was, like most football sackings, insensitive, brutal and heartless.

Even as Cruyff entered into 1995/96, despite struggling, Núñez failed to grasp how much the coach and more crucially, his philosophy had become an all-encompassing power within the club. By now, most Barca fans and the media were amazed he had been given another year. Cruyff, for his part, felt he had enough in the bank over eight years: the club's first European Cup, the European Cup Winners' Cup, the UEFA Super Cup, four league titles and a Copa Del Rey. As well as the trophies though, he had instilled something unique and special: principles, values and a way of playing.

Cruyff described his relationship with Núñez as purely business. He didn't trust his president. He always felt he had been installed 'to keep Núñez on the throne'. At Barcelona, after they had won the European Cup, Núñez and the vice-chairman Joan Gaspart (who was in charge of contracts) would appear, offering deals that Cruyff himself hadn't agreed to sanction. He would be better off away from those running the club at this point. Press conferences and post-match interviews from this time show Cruyff at his lowest; he sounds drained, frustrated, and flat. Cruyff wasn't without his faults either, as he remained headstrong and opinionated, and couldn't show weakness. He believed he could still turn it around.

What Cruyff would have observed from day one of his job is that being in power as president at FC Barcelona was like being the leader of a political party. Members collectively voted in a leader and the candidates appeared to spend most of their time on a campaign trail for re-election. A winning, entertaining side on the park was pivotal to maintaining power. Núñez would not have been used to a head coach talking to him the way Cruyff did. His demands to stay away from the dressing room would've eaten away at him.

The fans grew impatient with Cruyff's attempts to rebuild his team, while Núñez's plans to oust Cruyff gathered momentum. As the Dutchman toiled, and his support waned, Cruyff was of no use to Núñez. In his business dealings, Núñez was prudent and at that level, in the corporate world, would maintain a three-to five-year overview with recruitment in key areas. Núñez had already sounded out a replacement for his next head coach, in Bobby Robson. But with Cruyff, he wouldn't look beyond the subsequent two or three fixtures. Núñez was constantly gauging the reaction of the fans to see if he still had their support.

Cruyff wasn't a politician, he was a football man. His mentality was different. Football had to be played the correct way and winning should be regarded as a by-product of that. If they didn't win, they would find a way to win, eventually, and when they did they would sweep everyone aside just as the Dream Team had.

* * *

When those upstairs didn't get this, he would be quick to anger and had an unnerving ability to make authority figures look like gunslingers who showed up at the OK Corral with a water pistol. Whether it was Núñez, Ajax president Ton Harmsen or the beaks at the KNVB, when it came to standards and levels of expectation he was relentless and impatient and believed his team would eventually come good.

When it suited Núñez's ambitions to remain president, Cruyff would have soon served his purpose. Cruyff hoped football people would understand the cyclical nature of the game, but he was not given time to rebuild the way he wanted. It was pivotal that the board understood his long-term strategy. He sensed that Núñez was distancing himself and that animosity toward him from within the club began to grow.

By 1996 and the end of his tenure, suddenly there were problems. The president had an issue with Cruyff's son, Jordi, playing for the side. Jordi had come through the ranks and had to be better than everyone else. His father deliberately left the decision each year of his development to the coaches and managers as to whether they were keeping him. He had succeeded on his own. Then the medical staff had even turned against Cruyff. This annoyed him because he was always close to them and enjoyed looking through injuries and became quite the medical expert. He also wanted to sign a prospect from Bordeaux, but the board were reluctant and didn't rate him. That player was Zinedine Zidane.

With two games of the season left, and Bobby Robson rumoured to be on his way, vice-chairman Joan Gaspart decided to head into the dressing room to chat with Cruyff. When he tried to shake his hand, Cruyff called him a Judas and decried him for being a stooge for Núñez. Why couldn't he come down and do the dirty work? They started fighting, and Gaspart threatened to have him removed by police if he didn't leave the Nou Camp.

Gaspart has subsequently admitted he maybe shouldn't have gone to the dressing rooms to speak to Cruyff. Gaspart later recalled, 'Looking back on it, it was probably a mistake to go down to the dressing rooms and give him an explanation. It only made the situation worse. Things got violent – we both lost ourselves. We couldn't carry on after that, not even for two games.'

His shoddy treatment is now a sad part of the club's history and something Cruyff couldn't ever fully understand, particularly the timing: 'Why throw someone out just before the end of a competition?' When asked if he was angry at the management of Barca for sacking him, Cruyff was blunt, 'You could say that, yes. It was the way they did it. To destroy me as a person. You don't damage someone's reputation in order to fire them. You don't do that. Yes, I felt a lot of resentment.'

Over the years, once those running the club had moved on, Cruyff mellowed. Joan Laporta's appointment as president in 2003 was welcomed by most interested parties, but not all. Here was a president who seemed to behave more like a fan, with the club's best interests at heart. He would let the footballers and coaches get on with things; the perfect president for those on the footballing side of the business. There was some real optimism when Laporta was selected as he was prepared to ask questions and listen.

When he approached Cruyff, seeking advice about Barcelona's search for a coach and technical director, the Dutchman's response was simple. Frank Rijkaard and Txiki Begiristain were perfect for the job. Rijkaard brought Henk ten Cate and history would be made again over the resulting period.

In his autobiography, Cruyff begins a section with the sentence, 'My experience with football club directors has been a lot less fun.' If only Cruyff had been a little more forgiving, more versatile, even pretended to like his two presidents, how might it have panned out for him? He couldn't, though, as that was not part of his nature. That same headstrong personality made him join Feyenoord. He had to have the love, support and respect of his bosses. Both had to know their boundaries. Back or sack. Imagine if Laporta approached, and instead of asking for recommendations, asked him to be Barca coach? What a return that would've been – Cruyff bringing through and mentoring Pep Guardiola. When Rijkaard was sacked, Guardiola was promoted from within and played the same way, based on Cruyff's style. The club were back in great shape compared to how they were when he arrived as coach in 1988, with fans abandoning them and players so overloaded with fear they had started to play the ball backwards.

Despite delivering as a coach for both Ajax and Barcelona, those in charge were the reason why Cruyff's coaching career did break down. If he had been at both clubs when Michael van Praag and Joan Laporta were in charge, instead of Harmsen and Núñez, it could've been so much more workable. Presidents and directors moved too slowly for Cruyff, and player negotiations were far too protracted.

Cruyff acknowledged that he had an issue with directors. In his mind, footballers should be in control; people on the pitch should determine what the directors do and not the other way round. He once said, 'It's so important for football to remain under the control of footballers from the pitch upwards, right to the boardroom. Maybe it's a bit primitive but that's just how I think and that's why I've clashed with directors so often.'

Barcelona, under Laporta, had awarded Cruyff with an honorary president role. When Laporta's term as president was over, the club's members, the *socios*, voted in his successor, Sandro Rosell. He had been Laporta's running mate and vice-president. Laporta and Rosell had fallen out at the beginning of Frank Rijkaard's tenure when the new manager struggled to win matches; Rosell wanted him sacked. Rosell had worked as a Nike executive in Brazil and wanted to replace Rijkaard with Brazilian coach Luiz Felipe Scolari and change the direction of the club.

Rosell became upset when Laporta remained patient with Cruyff's recommendation, Rijkaard. Laporta also felt that with time, Rijkaard's side would improve. On Rosell's appointment, the first item on the agenda was to check if Cruyff's honorary position was awarded in line with the rules of the club. Cruyff was forced to resign from his post.

Rosell was involved in a court case centring around the transfer of Neymar from the Brazilian side Santos in 2013. Corruption charges were made after a Brazilian investment group claimed they received a far smaller compensation and that Neymar's full transfer fee was hidden by those involved. Rosell resigned as president in January 2014 because of these allegations, which he also vehemently denied.

Apropos of nothing, in 2017, Sandro Rosell was jailed without bail when he was caught up in a money-laundering investigation connected to buying television rights for matches featuring the Brazilian national side. Initially, Spanish prosecutors insisted on an 11-year sentence and a fine of 60m Euros. He was accused of forming part of a criminal organisation to help launder nearly 20m Euros. But on appeal, he was fully acquitted after 643 days.

Chapter 21

Dutch Legacy Influence …
Yet Never Dutch Coach

IT'S DIFFICULT to appreciate the depth of Cruyff's importance to his homeland and to Dutch football. 'Cruyff is a leader,' confirmed Ruud Gullit. 'Johan paved the way for us, van Basten, Rijkaard and myself. He put Holland on the international map of football with his brilliance.'

Johan Cruyff was the epitome of a Dutchman, full of aphorisms and sayings. Some were clear, some less so. He was a proud Amsterdammer, a fan of Ajax who made his debut for them aged 17; he and Rinus Michels worked wonders in raising the club's profile. He loved playing for his country and scored on his international debut for the Netherlands, aged 19, in the 1968 European Championship qualifiers. He was a confident footballer but had that additional X-factor to take him to the upper echelons of the greats of the game. As well as having a mission to spread the word of Total Football as a player, he took it one step further by becoming a successful coach.

Cruyff's exceptional performance and consistency at an elite level, on the world stage and over such a long period of time, was a major contributing factor to his enduring legacy. Yet the more successful he became, especially when he left Ajax for Barcelona, the more turmoil he seemed to cause, particularly with the KNVB.

He starred in the early 1970s Ajax team that were European champions three years in a row and became the best team in the world. He then moved to Barcelona, and, after a brief if misjudged early retirement, returned via the US and Spain to Ajax then finally, Feyenoord in the 1980s.

So, here we have someone who not only could play but looked the part. He was strong-willed and opinionated. The backdrop to his career, coming through in the liberal, free-thinking era at a time of hope, when people spoke up for change, seemed to help enhance this legend. It's obvious from the many games witnessed that he was one of the greatest footballers ever. He also had that determination, confidence and self-belief. On the pitch he would be a player, coach and referee. Yet the burning question remains: how was such an important figure to Dutch football not named manager of his country?

There was a natural point when the stars aligned for the 1990 World Cup in Italy. When Rinus Michels stepped down after winning the 1988 European Championships, Cruyff's former Feyenoord manager Thijs Libregts was named in his place. But after only two years in charge the players didn't think he was strong enough. They were successful and powerful, especially the three from AC Milan: Gullit, van Basten and Rijkaard. They got their way and Libregts was ousted. Those and other senior players decided they needed a firm hand and Libregts wasn't the man to lead them to glory. They wanted Cruyff.

This side were fresh from winning the Euros were arguably among the best players in the world, and held considerable power. They thought their preparation would cost them the chance of the World Cup. They were confident and at their peak and should've been heading to Italy as one of the favourites for the prize.

Cruyff had heard through the grapevine the job was his. He remained quiet, kept his cool, bided his time and waited, thinking he would be approached and offered the job. The players wanted him, the timing was right, and it seemed the perfect moment to take the reins. It seemed *too* perfect.

For Gullit, the 1988 success was based on the discipline and detail on and off the pitch from Michels. He knew Cruyff was cut from the same cloth and would be the answer coming into Italia '90. Gullit told an interview on Irish show *Off the Ball*, 'The biggest mistake we made was that we had a coach, Thijs Libregts, who was not up for it – we knew that. We had big problems with discipline, so there was a vote about it and then the whole team voted that there had to be a new coach and also the new coach had to be Johan Cruyff.'

So in the build-up to the tournament, players were distracted and attention focused on ousting Libregts and replacing him with Cruyff. It was Michels himself, by then a technical director at the KNVB, who offered the players a vote. The choices were Leo Beenhakker, Aad de Mos and Johan Cruyff. Most, but not all, voted for Cruyff, and his dream job didn't happen because Michels got nervous. He had heard that Cruyff had scores to settle and had plans to overthrow the KNVB. Michels was happy with how the national association was being run; he did not intend to cause any waves and wouldn't sanction the role. Michels over-ruled the players' choice and appointed his friend Leo Beenhakker instead.

Cruyff may have wanted his footballing people in place instead of the committee members who held the power but he didn't intend on restructuring the organisation. The KNVB – does the K and B stand for king and blazer? Michels could finally take his chance to put Cruyff in his place for some major felony, like refusing to take his coaching badges. Perhaps it's the petty and officious superpower they get when they don the blazer.

Cruyff would later openly admit that he thought the job was his. The reasons and rumours around the decision to overlook him ranged from a playing and coaching career spent at odds with the KNVB, to having not or ever intended to do his coaching badges. And the most far-fetched, which most Dutch football fans believe, was that Michels, having won the European Championship in 1988, didn't want Cruyff having the opportunity to eclipse him by winning the World Cup.

At this point, there was a tangible feeling that the Dutch felt they genuinely had the side to do it. The only thing missing was a big-name coach with the personality and vision to galvanise and set out his ideas. Being appointed meant Cruyff would have to ask Núñez for a six-week secondment from Barcelona. That, surprisingly, had been agreed. Ultimately, however, Beenhakker was cheaper, and a yes man, who wouldn't have needed to ask for the time. Clearly Michels was sick of Johan Cruyff and wanted someone who would wear the blazer.

When the players headed to Italy they spent more time arguing about Cruyff not being there as coach. With a terrible training camp in a deserted castle in Yugoslavia in the preparation, their discord and unhappiness was borne out in their performances. The most memorable Dutch moment of the tournament was not a wonder goal but Frank Rijkaard spitting on West Germany's Rudi Völler. It was a lack of discipline, the very thing Gullit feared. They struggled through the first round, drawing their three games against Egypt (1-1), England (0-0) and Ireland (1-1), and crashed out to West Germany in the round of 16 match.

Gullit fell out with Michels over the whole debacle and at one surreal point, they let rip at each other when they both wrote columns for rival newspapers. On reflection, Dutch football fans should have a sense of frustration and be aggrieved at missing out on such an extraordinary, once-in-a-lifetime opportunity, when Cruyff was desperate to manage them into a World Cup, on European soil. They could have easily won, and there's also a feeling football itself was cheated.

Cruyff had a career-long head-to-head with the Dutch football association and maybe they decided to opt for an easy life. His first argument was over money. When he started as an international, the players weren't paid. It was seen as a matter of honour to represent your nation. Cruyff was proud to do it, but not so happy when he found out other nations paid their players for appearing. He felt that it was unfair and he wanted his governing body to pay the players too. Even at this early age, he would be the self-appointed righter of wrongs, the shop steward, willing to go in and face the bosses and make his point.

In another altercation, Cruyff was furious when he heard the KNVB staff and officials were given insurance to fly but the players weren't. He had that changed too. Cruyff in so many situations was portrayed unfairly as the troublemaker, when he would say he was trying to improve the welfare of his colleagues. Instead of an instigator, he would've seen himself as a mediator and their representative.

As a player and more so as a manager, he was fond of what's referred to as the conflict model. This, when boiled down in layman's terms, was an approach which made the coach a homicidal psychopath if you annoyed him and didn't do what he demanded in training, or who you picked up during a corner. A real bollocking over the most trivial and unimportant matter to get a reaction would be frequent.

This approach was based on provoking people to a point where they wanted to fight. With their blood boiling and adrenalin pumping, they would be ready for war, or at least the tricky winger who waltzed around them in the first half. Most could handle it but Cruyff liked to do it to players, directors and club presidents, most of whom didn't appreciate or warrant it. He had made enemies throughout his career and football people have a tendency to remember and are unforgiving.

But Cruyff exhibited these traits too; easy to anger and stern when he felt wronged. For instance, when he headed off to Catalonia after losing the Ajax captaincy to Piet Keizer or his dispute with Núñez at Barcelona after failing to turn around the dismantled Dream Team in 1996. But perhaps there is no better example than when Ajax didn't extend his contract and he headed off to play for Feyenoord. A move entirely in keeping with his powerful and intense nature and personality.

As for the Dutch national job, Cruyff put it best in his autobiography, when he said, 'Michels was a man of extremes, who didn't make things easy for himself. Even though he cocked up the World Cup in 1990 for a great generation of footballers and for me I still have a warm feeling towards him.'

Chapter 22

Season 1983/84: Matchdays 24–28

WHAT BETTER way for Feyenoord to respond to the Groningen disappointment, their first defeat in 14 games, than to take on Ajax? The atmosphere in De Kuip was electric for De Klassieker; 58,000 eager fans showed up, and weren't let down. If the 'pension plan arrangement' deal was accurate, in this one game, Cruyff would have had 24,000 fans paying to see him.

Feyenoord opened the scoring with a glorious Ruud Gullit free kick. The goal is, quite rightly, often cited as one of the best ever scored in the Eredivisie. Playing outstanding football, Gullit showed why he, even at this young age, was a superstar in the making. It was one of those goals that the more you see it, the more implausible it becomes. From 36 yards out, Gullit placed a shot, with the inside of his foot, into the top corner.

The wonderful technique meant the power came from the speed and distance of the run-up. The free kick was taken more like a penalty. Questions could be raised about the positioning of Ajax's goalkeeper, Hans Galjé, but maybe on this occasion we should give the credit to Gullit for this wonderful goal, his 11th of an incredible season.

As if Gullit's opener wasn't enough to get the party started, Cruyff scored two minutes later. A short corner led to a quick pass to Gullit, who crossed into the box, where Cruyff leapt and his header was saved before he reacted and drove it in with his left foot from a few yards. Best of all, he celebrated with the full fist pump in the air, stretching and jumping in the distinctive goalscoring action he had used through the years. Perhaps it was a dig at Ajax, too old? Too fat? Really? I can't swear or curse in Dutch but his actions suggested the widely used expletive about going forth and multiplying.

Jan Mölby pulled one back early in the second half. A delightful Olsen cross from tight on the left was shouldered down by Rijkaard and Mölby forced it home. Cruyff then limped off after 75 minutes and was replaced by Zhelyaskov, before free-scoring midfielder André Hoekstra added his 14th of the season. When Gullit won the ball in midfield, he broke free into acres of space, strode into the box and cut back for Hoekstra to score with a left-footed shot from seven yards.

The fourth and final goal came in the 80th minute after Houtman fed in Henk Duut with a delightful reverse pass. Duut had only been on the pitch for three minutes having replaced Stanley Brard. He remained cool, passing a right-footed shot through the keeper's legs to clinch a 4-1 victory.

For matchday 25 and on a high, Feyenoord ventured to Deventer to face Go Ahead Eagles. Here are a few mildly interesting facts about Go Ahead Eagles. They once played Celtic in the European Cup Winners' Cup in 1965. Their away strip is green and white hoops. This was also Stein's first European tie and programmes are rare and valuable. Sadly, those anecdotes were more interesting than the game.

As the fixture unfolded, it looked as though this could be another Feyenoord slip-up or one of those scrappy days where champions-elect scrape out a point from the clutches of defeat. Or was this the slow disintegration of a side who assumed they were bound for glory and an unprecedented title?

The 16,000 crowd would witness a weird and wonderful Feyenoord show with Cruyff at the helm. Go Ahead Eagles took the lead in the second half with a Henk Veldmate goal on 68 minutes. However, Brard equalised six minutes later. Cruyff was battered and kicked even more than usual. And every time he was kicked there would be a huge cheer from the crowd. It was an untidy game on a hard, dry and bumpy pitch. Feyenoord would take the 1-1 draw and move on.

A difficult next match at home to AZ Alkmaar saw a 5-2 victory for Feyenoord. This would be the third of four 5-2 league scorelines. What does this score tell you? It says the defence are usually too busy attacking, meaning entertaining and scoring goals is the preferred option. In this particular game, Houtman scored a hat-trick with the other goals coming from defenders Wijnstekers and Duut.

The match followed a familiar pattern with Feyenoord conceding first as Alkmaar's Ricky Talan opened the scoring after six minutes. Houtman equalised two minutes later, before scoring his second after 35 minutes.

With the score sitting at 2-1 going into the break the game was still in the balance. Feyenoord knew they needed to up the tempo to secure the win and their fans must've been wondering what side would show up in the second half.

Houtman calmed proceedings with his 15th goal of the season when he completed his hat-trick after 61 minutes. Wijnstekers scored the fourth in the 65th minute before AZ Alkmaar's Berte van der Poppe pulled one back two minutes later. Duut secured the 5-2 win after 70 minutes.

The games this season were overloaded with goals and excitement. If not full of quality, they pulsated with explosive moments and entertaining contests. They mixed ferocious tackling and long balls with brief and compelling moments of brilliance as teams slugged it out. It was a fascinating aspect of the 1983/84 campaign. Some would expect refinement and quality but sometimes it was all-out attacking football, resulting in high-scoring games. When you look at the number of goals per game, scores like 5-2, 4-1 and 7-2 were not uncommon, and even the freakish 8-2 against Ajax (freakish because no matter how an 8-2 score can look, the game was more balanced than that. It was the most 'un-8-2' 8-2 trouncing you could ever witness). The Dutch league was goal crazy across the season with 1,079 goals scored in total.

Matchday 27 saw a bumper crowd of 28,000 show up at the Philips Stadion to watch Cruyff's Feyenoord take on PSV. The Eindhoven side were on an incredible run of form having only lost once in 20 games before suffering a shock defeat to Go Ahead Eagles. Again, the home fans booed Cruyff every time he touched the ball. That's football, eh? They say it's respect, but it means they know you're the main man. Feyenoord took the lead in the 29th minute when Cruyff got past his marker and crossed to Houtman, who laid it back for Duut to drive a low, right-footed shot past Hans Segers. It was the defender's fifth goal of the season.

This was an exciting, open game, flowing from end to end with brilliant goalkeeping on display from both sides. Hiele, in particular, made some wonderful saves, one especially from a perfectly met Michel Valke left-foot rocket from 35 yards. PSV's Koolhof also hit the post with a spectacular Marco van Basten-style volley.

Feyenoord failed to ensure a clean sheet and missed out on the win, maybe thinking that they had the points in the bag. Again, the damage was done when they lost Cruyff, who had to limp off in the 73rd minute, to be replaced by Willy Carbo.

To the untrained eye, it looked like Cruyff had made his own decision and decided he'd had enough and was walking off. However, it was something he always did. A constant part of his game, when he played wide, was remaining in communication with the coaching staff, asking what they wanted from him – and what he could tell the players. He may have been the de facto coach on the pitch and have organised and shaped the team but he wouldn't be disrespectful publicly to his coach unless he deserved it.

It was astonishing that he was able to get through so many games unscathed, especially given the treatment he received. He was central to everything Feyenoord did. Most of the play started with him and as such a pivotal player he would be a target for opponents.

PSV's pressure paid off when Erik-Jan van den Boogard headed on to Glenn Hysén. The Swedish defender, who would later join Liverpool, looped a header home for the equaliser for PSV with three minutes remaining.

Feyenoord marched out of matchday 28 closing in on a historic title with a 5-2 home win against Roda in front of 20,931 fans. Untidy defending allowed Feyenoord the opener when Roda failed to clear a cross and Cruyff cut it back for Gullit, who scored with a powerful drive through a crowded box. After the half-hour mark, Roda's hard work paid off and they came back into the game with a well-placed John Eriksen header, only to concede two minutes later when Hoekstra scored his 17th of the season. Sjaak Troost drove from defence down the right wing and pulled back a great cross for Hoekstra to head home. Two minutes later, however, Roda equalised again through Hexham-born Englishman Chris Guthrie.

Gullit provided the third with some wonderful wing play, getting around Roda's jumbled-up full-back and crossing in for Houtman to score with a header after 40 minutes – meaning an average scoring rate of one goal every eight minutes. It was hardly reassuring, measured and calming football. But then again, this wasn't an ordinary season.

After 53 minutes, Hoekstra continued a brilliant season with his 18th goal before Ivan Nielsen scored on the 90th minute, to make the final score 5-2. Cruyff had earlier missed a great chance when the ball fell to him in the six-yard box and Gullit had been imperious at times.

Chapter 23

Homage to Catalonia
Part 1: La Masia

*'Johan Cruyff painted the chapel, and Barcelona
coaches since, merely restore or improve it.'*
Pep Guardiola

IN JANUARY 1988, on hearing the faintest whisper that
Johan Cruyff had started to consider leaving his job at Ajax,
Barcelona-based journalist Joan Patsy headed to Amsterdam
sensing no doubt that this was a career-defining scoop. He
didn't know it at the time but his life and career would, in the
fullness of time, change from this point on. He would become
a close friend and then an adviser, working alongside Cruyff
when he eventually joined Barcelona some months later.

Before he met Cruyff, Joan Patsy had a normal, happy life.
Let's rewind, though, to a cold and bitter winter's day. The writer
and his photographer Jaume Amor headed to Cruyff's home in
the outskirts of Amsterdam, in Vinkeveen, on 5 January 1988.
After much convincing, they finally got by a sympathetic Mrs
Cruyff and eventually managed to get in out of the cold and
were offered a cup of tea. They were in. They were surprised at

how friendly and relaxed everything was and see Cruyff, jovial and on the phone. He waved at the pair and beckoned them in. 'I won't comment on this move, but we can talk a bit if you like,' he said. Then Cruyff proceeded to discuss, at length, what he thought was wrong with the side, and, what he would do if he did become a coach.

The visitors were mesmerised. Patsy would later explain, 'Before I met Johan, my life was fine,' while ruefully considering the impact the coach would have on him. 'But from the moment I met him, my life took on a new dimension. In many different ways. Johan taught me a lot of things I could apply to my own life and which helped in my personal development.'

Cruyff had been watching Barcelona's games from afar. In seconds he could see one fundamental problem for the team. In the chat, Cruyff explained that the goalkeeper was in the wrong starting position. If he stood out one metre more, the problems in the penalty area would be solved. Such were the fine margins and minor-seeming details he would be on top of.

On 4 May 1988, Johan Cruyff was named Barcelona coach. The club hadn't won LaLiga in 14 years but he would go on to win 11 trophies over eight years, including four league titles in a row, and finally, in 1992, the club's Holy Grail of winning the European Cup by beating Sampdoria at Wembley. Not only did Cruyff transform Barcelona, but he also revolutionised the game itself.

On his return to the club as a coach, Cruyff developed what would become known as his Dream Team. Former player and team-mate Antonio de la Cruz summed it up perfectly, 'Barcelona gave Cruyff the opportunity to put his footballing philosophy into practice. And there you had the example, in the famous Dream Team, that won consecutive titles. So Johan and the club's ideals became inseparable, they were synonymous with each other.' They even managed a famous 5-0 victory over Real Madrid which delighted the Catalans.

Rejoining Barcelona, Cruyff was initially excited to oversee a huge project as a coach to a club steeped in technically gifted players who only played attacking football. But he would be disappointed. Where was the passion, excitement and belief? He wanted players to connect with the fans, he wanted energy and excitement but found he had to coax his side to play without fear. 'Every player in Amsterdam thought about attacking, while everyone in Barcelona played backwards. So I had to start by changing their pattern of thought,' he said.

At Ajax as a player and coach, everyone ate, drank and slept football. Football was all-encompassing and it meant everything. At Barcelona, no one did. But Cruyff would soon have them chatting and playing.

As a former Barca player, it was a little easier. He knew what to expect and was aware of the politics and responsibility of representing more than a club. This was a cause. He also understood the Catalan way; their mentality and distinct character. He was in classic Cruyff mode; the elements which made him peerless as a player, that fierce genius, came out in his interviews. On top of the now infamous 'know your place' comments to Núñez, and a general broadside to those upstairs to stay away from the football, elsewhere, to the media and fans, he made the club more accessible. Fans were allowed in to watch the team training; the press were given wider access. He knew he needed to reconnect with the supporters.

Cruyff started on the training ground. He would vary sessions, encouraging and driving his players. He would tell the striker that he was the first defender. The goalkeeper was the first attacker. He restructured the side, had them fitter and coached them in his style. The training was doubled and made more intense. Coaching was detailed; about metres and distances. Defenders were made to work harder. To play his way you had to be faster, the players listened and it worked. He changed their thinking about space on the pitch, and started to iron out minor mistakes.

Sometimes Cruyff would sit on a ball on the sidelines to watch the team train. Passers-by would think he was in the middle of a daydream. If he watched at this level, he noticed those little things such as spotting when a defender's starting position was a few metres out, or seeing positional problems others wouldn't see. Triangles were everywhere in his thinking. Three men; one would be passing and the others creating options with their run. Eleven men in motion. Constant passing, circulating and moving the ball.

Perhaps Cruyff himself didn't know the extent the club had plummeted to. It wasn't only the team's performance, but the coaching, the youth setup, the staff and the whole infrastructure. He slowly realised how colossal the job was, and that he needed time to do it.

When he left as a player in 1979, he pleaded with and then demanded that the Barcelona board overhaul and make more of their youth set up. The original La Masia (Catalan for 'farmhouse') was modernised and extended to include a dormitory. It looks like a seminary or a monastery but the religion here is Barcelona and a way of playing football, within the doctrine, rules and belief systems of the club. Cruyff is often credited with setting up La Masia but he had advised Núñez in 1979 and when he returned in 1988, he insisted on developing and nurturing talent from the youth academy. So the infrastructure was improved as well as tactical organisation.

Youth development has always been part of the club. Barcelona's first foray into youth football can be traced back to 1901 when a second team was created. A third and fourth team would later follow, and a structure was beginning to be slowly set in place. Even then, the club's identity was prevalent and the guiding principle was simple: attacking, possession-based football which has remained a tenet throughout the club's history. Other significant dates would include 1918, when the board of founder Joan Gamper actively pushed and encouraged the formation of children and youth teams. Then, in 1961, Enric Llaudet, the son of a wealthy industrialist, had inherited the family's textile business. When he was president from 1961 to 1968, he found the club in huge debt. He was voted in after promising to push and develop a residential youth academy. Llaudet brought in club legend László Kubala to oversee the youth setup. He was soon promoted to head coach then, in 1963, the academy had to close due to financial problems.

With the structure now in place, what they needed was a defined approach. The evolution of Barcelona's unique style of play always garners the same headline names like Rinus Michels, Johan Cruyff and Pep Guardiola but like any football club, its crucial figures like Joan Vila, Paco Seirul·lo and Laureano Ruiz bring it together. Ruiz had been setting his methods in place with the youth setup since his appointment in 1972. His sides were coached to master a unique style and this would be crucial to Cruyff's football vision. Ruiz had set in place training methods and the same tactical plan and shape with every team. He also felt it was important to educate and develop the players as people too.

La Masia was operational but not as central to the club as it should've been. It had become an afterthought and was often the last thing discussed at meetings. When it did function, its priority, rather unbelievably, was to make sure players coming through were tall enough – the minimum height was 1.8m (just under 5ft 11in). It wasn't a football academy so much as a police academy. Players had to have the physique to withstand the pressure of making it in the first team or they were released.

As a result, those coming through weren't competent enough and too many smaller players were forced to leave. That had to change. Cruyff, perhaps speaking from personal experience, realised he was always picked upon because of his height and slender build when he was younger. He had to prove that he could play. He wanted players who were comfortable on the ball, who had a great first touch, and height was irrelevant. If they were quick enough and could read the game, that was enough. Cruyff explained, 'I had short lads like Albert Ferrer, Sergi or Guillermo Amor, players without great physiques but who pampered the ball with their touch and pressed the opposition like rats. Even Pep wasn't all that physically but with the ball he was intelligent. That's what I wanted.'

This was the original academy. The setting has now changed but the intent remains. The youth academy moved to the state-of-the-art training complex, Barcelona's Ciutat Esporta Joan Camper, named after the club's founder. The site opened in 2018 with the same focus and purpose, football which was based around possession, pressing and positioning and the improbable task of bringing through the next Messi, Iniesta and Xavi.

This, more than any European Cup or La Liga title, was perhaps Cruyff's most important legacy to Barcelona. Here, players were allowed to develop from childhood into adulthood with football and academic focuses, as they were in the classroom too. Here they would also learn the football philosophy and what it meant to wear a Barcelona shirt.

The building itself was used as a logistical base during the construction of the Nou Camp. Then it became the main administrative HQ of the club but when they moved out, it was left lying empty. In July 1979, the *socios* (club members) voted in favour of plans to refurbish the farmhouse as a residential football school. The dormitory was extended and a stadium for Barca B and the youth sides was constructed.

In 1979, though, president Núñez headed a group including Juan Amat as head of youth football (he would soon leave after a fall-out) and director of methodology Joan Vila. Vila, along with Paco Seirul·lo, was a chief proponent of the core Barcelona style that the world came to love – a pressing game of possession and tiki-taka. He brought through Puyol, Xavi and Iniesta among many others. He was sacked by the club in 2018. Then there was the renowned talent spotter Oriol Tort Martinez. This was the official era of the residential youth academy, with players who lived outside a daily commute, staying in the farmhouse.

Cruyff incorporated the principles set in place by Michels then Juvenil A coach Luareneo Luiz, who was pivotal to the style of the modern Barcelona we know. He, in effect, set in place the key points: the shape across each of Barca's 13 sides would be a 3-4-3. Smaller players, if technically proficient would be brought in. Focus was on their first touch, when they lost the ball, they pressed high. This was uniform throughout each side. Cruyff rolled all of these practices out while he was coach. He also implemented his favourite drill, the rondo, now used by most football teams across the globe. 'Everything that goes on in a match, except shooting, you can do in a rondo,' explained Cruyff. 'The competitive aspect, fighting to make space, what to do when in possession and what to do when you haven't got the ball, how to play 'one touch' soccer, how to counteract the tight marking and how to win the ball back.

By 2010, La Masia provided ten of the players who won the World Cup for Spain. In November 2012, the late Tito Vilanova brought this to a perfect conclusion when he played 11 homegrown players from La Masia, on the pitch at the same time, against Levante. Lionel Messi, Cesc Fabregas, Xavi and Andres Iniesta all played.

Cruyff wanted to develop players but it was mainly about the philosophy and the way they played rather than the results they achieved. Guardiola believed that the biggest victory was to give a La Masia player their debut. In his reign as head coach, he gave 28 players from the youth academy their first-team breakthroughs.

It was a structured, detailed process, and only a long-term coaching approach to drills and fitness would allow it to work. For all his skill and the complexity of how he would want the game played, Cruyff was a great believer that players needed to work on the basics like controlling with the chest, passing, how to receive possession, working on the weaker foot, heading, and learning how to pass the ball correctly. The complexity and shape of Total Football meant nothing unless you won the ball, as without it you couldn't win matches.

Chapter 24

Here's Looking at Euclid

CRUYFF WAS often compared to a mathematician. David Miller, former chief sportswriter of *The Times*, described him as 'Pythagoras in Boots'. When you consider how pivotal triangles, time, speed, distance, angles and space were to him, it's inevitable the comparisons would emerge. The best coaches tend to have a complex, mathematical system, one of angles, patterns, shape and form.

The players are crucial; they add movement, discipline and technique. They work collectively, keep possession and press hard to win the ball back. The players may change but the system remains. The coach's job is then to get the message embedded in the mind of the players and ensure they can understand how to implement instructions.

Top managers across the years like Jock Stein, Matt Busby, Bill Shankly and Alex Ferguson, and the modern ones like Jurgen Klopp and Pep Guardiola, found success by tweaking the smallest details. They also added something unique that outwitted their opponent. It might be extreme; a world record transfer for one of the best goalkeepers, or a centre-half. Better still, they might see something in an under-appreciated player already on their staff and by improving their fitness, giving them renewed confidence, suddenly an average player is turned into a world-beater. They must play within the system though or it doesn't work. Something as simple as adding a little creativity, with the player who can make that pass, can result in a legend being made.

Then you have coaches who use motivation, mind games and demand effort, and those who like repetition and simplicity. Alex Ferguson found success, winning the treble in the late 1990s, with 4-4-2; he kept it simple. Two fast and creative wingers supplying two scorers and two midfielders who relentlessly worked for the team. It was as much about the opposition as it was their own game. Identifying a weakness and playing some mind games.

The old-school approach got them so far but at Wembley, in the Champions League Final of 2011, Barcelona just didn't defeat Manchester United 3-1, they comprehensively beat the team and the club's ethos, forcing them to rethink how the game should be played. By 2013, Ferguson had retired and the club, some seven years later, are still toiling.

When Jock Stein's Celtic became the first British side to win the European Cup, in Lisbon in 1967, he out-witted the best coach in the world at the time, Inter's Helenio Herrera. When Stein watched upcoming opposition, he used a piece of paper with the shape of the pitch on it and with his pen, as he watched, he copied and marked the movement of the ball. This way he could see where the ball had been most, and work out where the danger would come from. Sometimes he would be left with a blob, and other times he would be left with pristine mathematical triangles, patterns and forms, angles, and diamond shapes.

Stein, like Cruyff, believed football was about entertaining the fans. It was about excitement and attacking play. For instance, Celtic used high wingers who would fall back allowing full-backs Tommy Gemmell and Jim Craig to gallop forward and overlap. Stein didn't want to just win games, he drove his players to destroy any opposition they faced, to score and win, the 'Celtic Way'.

Finding a fitting comparison to adequately compare Cruyff's impact on his sport is not easy. But perhaps a suitable comparison is a basketball coach, the Zen Master, Phil Jackson, with his Triangle Offense at Chicago Bulls. Jackson created the system to satisfy and keep the rest of his group of superstars happy, and incorporate more of a team ethic. Due to the focus and pressure being placed on Michael Jordan, the Triangle Offense allowed the team's responsibility to be shared, rather than asking Jordan to shoulder it.

Cruyff's Total Football and Jackson's triangle were systems handed down and tweaked. In Cruyff's case, it was the Hogan-Austria-Hungary-Michels lineage. For Jackson, according to an article in the *New York Times* by Dan Barry, his system had been around for a while: 'The Triangle Offense was born on the hardwood courts of the University of Southern California in the 1940s, the offspring of the university's innovative basketball coach, Justin McCarthy "Sam" Barry.'

The system would be popularised by former University of South California player Tex Winter, while he coached at

Houston and Northwestern. Winter was an assistant at Chicago from 1985. When Jackson got the chance to join the staff at the Chicago Bulls as an assistant coach in 1987, Winter was on the staff there. He would find success with the system when Winter and Jackson later moved to LA Lakers.

So the triangle lineage goes Sam Barry-Tex Winter-Phil Jackson. Both Cruyff and Jackson have never claimed the systems, they have only been heavily attributed with popularising and widely implementing them. With Jackson's Triangle Offense and Cruyff's Total Football, the systems were only as good as the players they had available to play them. It's easy to play them with Michael Johnson, Scottie Pippen, Kobe Bryant or Shaquille O'Neal – or in Cruyff's case, Guardiola, Laudrup or Stoichkov.

John Coltrane and Johan Cruyff redefined jazz music and football respectively. Some would argue that they elevated both to a superior level by shifting and resetting their respective genres.

Perhaps a better example in terms of making a game-changing sporting moment would be the impact high jumper Dick Fosbury had on his sport. When he won the gold medal in Mexico in 1968, he brought the world's attention to his method and soon everyone applied the Fosbury Flop.

Cruyff's football methodology was one of big ideas but his vision could only be perfected if mistakes were eradicated. And mistakes tended to be marginal and trivial and occur more commonly at the back.

Chapter 25

Season 1983/84:
Matchdays 29–34

MATCHDAY 29 and Feyenoord were due to play away at local rivals SBV Excelsior Rotterdam. The casual observer and those with a keen eye for detail would be taking a second look while poring over this one as the game was actually played at De Kuip. We can only assume due to demand, with Feyenoord going for the championship and Cruyff coming to what could be the end of an amazing season, that common sense took hold and the local derby match was switched to allow more spectators in?

It's only an eight-minute drive from De Kuip to Woudestein, home of SBV Excelsior Rotterdam. Excelsior have one of the smallest stadiums in Dutch football though it is a charming ground. With the match switched, 19,130 were able to see Feyenoord in their yellow away shirts take on Excelsior, away – at home.

Cruyff was playing well and performing to the gallery, displaying a vast array of tricks, moves and link-up play. When he played an excellent long curving pass with the outside of his right foot to Henk Duut in the Excelsior box, the big defender was tripped, and the referee awarded a rare penalty. Again, it was Peter Houtman who stepped up to take care of business, scoring from the spot after 69 minutes.

Three minutes later, Cruyff played a one-two with Hoekstra before setting up Houtman for his second. The points were in the bag.

For matchday 30, Feyenoord welcomed neighbours Sparta Rotterdam to De Kuip, but the game ended in a goalless draw. As it was Easter weekend and the game played on Good Friday, a bumper crowd of 35,897 turned out to see the derby. This was Feyenoord's only 0-0 draw in the league campaign. The well-defined and recognised Feyenoord way, especially this season, was one of scoring and conceding so the goalless scoreline was unusual.

However, in the same round of fixtures, on week 30, Feyenoord's nearest rivals PSV and Ajax played each other and also drew 0-0, both failing to capitalise on the leaders' slip-up. No doubt Cruyff would've remained upbeat, considering it another hard-earned point and driving his team-mates on to a title-winning run-in. Feyenoord remained on top.

Forensic analysis of the Eredivisie table and the form of the three title challengers tells its own story. Feyenoord had won five and drawn one of their previous six games to take 11 points from a possible 12. PSV had won four, drawn one and lost one for a return of nine points. Ajax's record makes grim reading with three draws and one defeat, and just two wins for a tally of seven points.

In football, in a title chase, no game can ever be taken for granted or described as easy but on matchday 31, Easter

Sunday, Feyenoord travelled to Dordrecht to take on a DS'79 side languishing at the bottom of the league. Locals present witnessed a man of the match performance as Cruyff scored twice, laid on one and nudged his team closer to the championship with four games remaining.

Cruyff was in the mood and the sun shone as he passed the ball with the outside of the foot, and tried audacious chip shots. At one point, he took a throw-in and launched it in like a corner into the six-yard box, forcing the keeper to come out to snatch it. When Gullit was fouled on the right, on one of the free kicks, Cruyff crossed the ball, well it was more like a pass, straight on to the head of Ben Wijnstekers, who opened the scoring after 27 minutes.

Dick van der Starre, the DS goalkeeper, was too slack feeding the ball out to his team-mate, who fluffed his lines. Cruyff chased it down, the ball broke to Hoekstra, who played it back to his colleague to finish with the outside of the right foot and make it 2-0 ...

Cruyff then had a powerful left-footed shot from 25 yards out, forcing a great save from van der Starre. His second goal was vintage Cruyff. He picked the ball up deep, passed to Gullit accelerated to receive the return pass before advancing into the box, taking it round the keeper and calmly placing it in the net to confirm a 3-0 win. In these two back-to-back games, the 37-year-old Cruyff played well, especially on Easter Sunday, covering every blade of grass and expending so much energy. The repercussions of these two fixtures will make a dramatic return later in our story.

With three games left, Feyenoord welcomed Utrecht on a sunny but extremely blustery day. The excitement must've been building as another whopper of a crowd of 31,038 showed up, finally starting to believe. It is crude to talk about money, but equally it is remiss not to cover the topic, such was the nature of Cruyff's final season at Feyenoord and his wages based on gate receipts.

By applying some rudimentary arithmetic and rough guesstimates, in this arrangement, Feyenoord kept the average gate of 10,000, plus 1,000, then Cruyff and the club halved the remainder. This meant that Cruyff was receiving payment from approximately 10,000 paying customers. Now, even if they were paying as little as £3 per person, £30,000 in 1984 is worth, according to a reputable financial website's inflation calculator, around £97,000. That's a conservative estimation. No wonder Johan hardly missed a shift. He missed one league game in the season, and Feyenoord were beaten, against Groningen in February.

Utrecht were under the cosh from kick-off. Wijnstekers was a powerful and athletic left-back who could run relentlessly, and as such, linked up constantly with Cruyff. He set him up early on in the game, withstood a nasty challenge from behind which would have received a red card today, and, staying on his feet, whipped in a left-footed strike which went wide.

The goal finally came in the second half when, on 59 minutes, Cruyff took a quick free kick and passed inside to van de Korput who launched a hopeful ball into the box. It seemed to get caught in the wind, the defender misjudged the flight and Stanley Brard reacted quickly, winning the ball and cutting it back from the left for Gullit to put into an empty goal and bring up his 14th of the season.

The second goal summed up Cruyff's season at Feyenoord in one move. He took a corner on the left with the outside of his right foot and Gullit rose to head in. He met the cross perfectly to score a great goal.

It was classy and clinical. It was simple but with that corner and header, it was football of the highest level, and emphatically effective.

The third goal came in the last minute of the game. The fans were restless and breaking down fences to get through and on to the pitch. Cruyff brought the ball down in the box and killed it in one touch, before playing it to midfielder Hoekstra to finish from 12 yards out, with his 19th goal of the season. At 3-0, fans started invading the pitch, and Cruyff ran off before the crowd ratcheted up the mania. Cruyff had brought something special to their season and now it was actually happening.

It was top versus second bottom for matchday 33 with Feyenoord facing Willem II in the penultimate league fixture of the season. Feyenoord could seal the Eredivisie title with a win. In an old-fashioned stadium, flags were placed around the perimeter walls. Cruyff was starting to have fun, spraying long crosses from deep-lying positions. He played in Hoekstra early on, who nearly opened the scoring.

When Gullit picked the ball up, he only had one thing on his mind and that was to find Cruyff, which he did, playing it into the box with the outside of his right foot. It fell to the 37-year-old, who scored his tenth of the season just 13 minutes into the game. Gullit then took a wander down the right-hand side and burst into space, lost his marker, then expertly tried to chip the keeper. He had obviously been watching Cruyff.

Before half-time, Hoekstra won the ball in the middle and played it wide to Gullit. With Willem's keeper Jan Formannoy looking all at sea attempting to intercept and punch the cross, it was left for Henk Duut to score with the header, into an empty net for his sixth goal of the season, to make it 2-0.

Then, when Cruyff played it wide, instead of standing and wondering at its perfection, he ran through and, when he received the ball back, chipped it. The ball hit the bar, and it fell to Houtman, who was in for the third goal.

The excitement got too much for the visiting Feyenoord fans, and a mass invasion ensued; it remained good-humoured and confined. They self-policed before evolving into something resembling a massive conga. Inevitably, the ref had to stop play until they left the pitch. Cruyff had to plead with fans to allow the game to finish, pointing at his wrist as if to say 'there's loads of time left, we need to finish this'. The followers listened to their messiah.

Eventually, they congregated around the perimeter as if watching a game in a public park. When Cruyff played in Houtman in 79 minutes, Formannoy parried it, and the ball fell to Stanley Brard. When he put in the fourth, it was a delicious cocktail of mayhem and bedlam. Brard was practically trampled over and players were forced to scarper again and head off the pitch.

Play eventually resumed and when Gullit and Cruyff linked up, it was Cruyff who was through and ready to score the fifth, but the keeper's save fell to Houtman who added his 20th goal of the season. Cruyff and his team-mates were seen sprinting off the park. Gullit made it through eventually.

The league was won. It was time for the classic shot of the club coaches, carrying the team, and directors, and family with police outriders, back to Rotterdam for a civic reception of brass bands and oompah bands. The team were on the balcony in front of thousands of adoring Feyenoord fans. Cruyff watched on quietly. He'd seen this plenty of times before, no doubt enjoying and savouring the moment and glad it would soon be over. He had put in another top-level performance, admittedly against weaker opposition, but he still delivered.

It was another great game, despite the pandemonium and the fans going crazy. Cruyff looked reserved and reflective in the video footage after what was his ninth Dutch title, to go with his Barcelona championship from 1973/74. He may have been considering that this was the end, and secretly considering how earlier in the week he had won the Dutch Cup. Now, he was officially going out winning the double. It was a far more fitting re-write and ending to the quite extraordinary tale which started back on 15 November 1964. Being a professional footballer, he may have been thinking no more running, sprints, or cross country and rigorous pre-season training camps.

On 12 May, the final game of the season saw an expectant crowd of 33,263 show up to celebrate winning the Dutch title and say goodbye to Cruyff. The champions faced FC Zwolle '82 and De Kuip was in a jubilant mood. Looking at the footage, there seems like many more than 33,000 made it to the game. I could be wrong, as Feyenoord's ground then was a big space. It should be highlighted that across football in this era, from the 1970s and the 1980s, that official attendances were notoriously inaccurate. It was one of the worst kept secrets in football. Clubs would have an official attendance but it was rarely anywhere close to the correct number.

In the days before games were ticketed, and electronic passes and turnstiles were in place, fans could just show up and many jumped the turnstiles (like I did to see Cruyff against Celtic). On some occasions, there could be another 10,000 over the official club attendance. The rules regarding attendances have changed and clubs, quite rightly, have to comply with the law.

The familiar move; Gullit to Cruyff to Hoekstra, came close to yielding an early goal but the season's familiar pattern continued with Feyenoord conceding four minutes into the game when Zwolle took an early lead. René IJzerman drove forward and played it wide to Johnny Rep, who chipped in a delicious cross for Alex Booy to score with a looping header from 12 yards.

Gullit caused no end of problems down the right and he soon came inside, finding Cruyff with a perfectly placed left-footed pass. The movement and timing were perfect. Cruyff arrived at the right place at the right time, and with the slightest first touch he killed and arced the ball around the advancing keeper to score his 11th league goal of the season after 13 minutes.

Cruyff was everywhere in this game and eventually, on 76 minutes, he finally unlocked the door. Taking a pass from Hoekstra, he fed through to Gullit who played it inside to Peter Houtman for his 21st goal of the season. The star of the show was substituted in the 79th minute and given the chance to take a bow and applause from the crowd.

On the final whistle, Cruyff remained surprisingly modest, perhaps relieved. His team-mates Ben Wijnstekers and Stanley

Brard raised him on their shoulders. He stayed dignified, quite cool and respectful, and headed off up the tunnel. He was filmed doing the long walk through the inner sanctum of the stadium, and upstairs to the dressing rooms. TV cameras and press photographers followed him into the changing room, where he stripped to his shorts and socks and enjoyed a beer. He was still in great shape and not fat, as Ajax tried to claim. There was hardly an extra ounce. He was lean and in the shape of a 26-year-old, smiling as he tossed his boots across the tiled floor. Meanwhile, the cameramen got a chance for their final shot of the Dutch superstar ending one of the greatest careers in the history of the sport (Cruyff would play one more game, in Saudi Arabia when Feyenoord played Al-Ahli, scoring and providing an assist, to bring the curtain down on an amazing career).

In the end, Feyenoord won the title with 57 points and qualified for the European Cup. PSV were second on 52 and Ajax third on 51, both qualifying for the UEFA Cup. Since Feyenoord had won the double, Fortuna Sittard, the runners-up in the KNVB final, took their place in the European Cup Winners' Cup. But what you must truly ask yourself, and it is a simple question – if Ajax kept Cruyff and had been playing his final year there, would they have won the league and cup double?

Chapter 26

Here's ... Johnny

AFTER HIS successful double-winning season in Feyenoord and, significantly, his fifth Dutch Player of the Year award, Cruyff retired having made his point with a stark reminder to his one true love, Ajax, that they should've renewed his contract. After this year, Feyenoord tried to extend his stay with them but Cruyff was done.

Feyenoord tried to stick with the formula and the following season they lined up another ageing Dutch football legend, also an ex-Ajax player, Johnny Rep. Rep unsurprisingly, despite being a wonderfully stylish and elegant footballer, couldn't quite manage to repeat Cruyff's feats. Feyenoord did not maintain their form. They were beaten in the lucrative European Cup and struggled in the league. Trying to 'do a Cruyff' proved far more difficult than Cruyff made it look. It was like the Beach Boys when they sent the band on tour with Bruce Welch as lead singer – and made Brian Wilson, the genius, stay at home to record the music and make hits. Greatness isn't easily replaced.

Rep did not get on too well with Cruyff, not at first anyway, and not in 1973 either when he had voted to oust him as captain.

'I had problems with Johan,' confirmed Rep. 'We did not get along well, except on the ground. I was a little bit young and Johan was always telling me what to do. Do this, do that. And I was a boy but I spoke back to him. He was stubborn and so was I – that was our problem. And Johan doesn't like that. You must always say ok. But I did it instinctively because I didn't like him telling me what to do.' Rep was merely sticking up for himself and behaving the way Cruyff would be if the roles were reversed.

Rep was a glorious part of the 1970s Dutch team alongside Cruyff, Neeskens and Krol. He looked the essence of a cool 1970s football star playing with a confidence and swagger. He had the rock 'n' roll image and was a fantastic player with flair, pace and power. Arguably, he was Keith Richards to Mick Jagger's Cruyff. The principle of Total Football is centred around the entire team, yet Rep, Johan Neeskens and Cruyff were like the Holy Trinity of the philosophy and the most instrumental in furthering it.

His personality was unlike Cruyff's though. Whereas Cruyff didn't care who he upset, believing if everyone did what he wanted to do then the team would win, Rep preferred to be one of the lads and get on with everyone. He wasn't trying to reinvent the genre. Feyenoord had enough issues to contend with, and it would be impossible to maintain the same on-field performance levels. Sides also knew how Feyenoord were set up to play.

Maybe the rest of his team-mates suffered from not having Cruyff coaching and guiding them on the park. Ruud Gullit could play anywhere. At his first club, Amsterdam DWS, he started at centre-half. It was his attacking forays which caught the eye and saw him sign for Haarlem. He played at centre-half for the first season but in his second he was moved into midfield. When Cruyff arrived, the elder statesman recognised his versatility and played him on the right wing. He was adamant that it was Gullit's best position. When Cruyff was no longer there, Gullit would have felt he had to move back to support and was missing that guidance.

Johnny Rep is still the leading Dutch goalscorer at the World Cup finals having scored four goals in 1974 and three in 1978. In the World Cup games, he played as a right-sided striker. He was a colourful, entertaining player, tearing down the wing, terrorising and confusing opponents.

Rep scored the goal that kept the Dutch in the 1978 tournament, in the same game that Archie Gemmill entered folklore with his famous solo goal. Rep dropped deep, taking the ball from Neeskens and moving into space before belting a ferocious shot that rocketed past Alan Rough. The goal saved the Dutch. Yet Rep was modest and would later describe it thus, 'A little bit of a lucky goal.' Yes, lucky and heartbreaking – especially if you were Scottish.

In 1984, though, he was coming to Feyenoord after a colourful and creative career which saw him move from Ajax, Valencia, Bastia, Saint Etienne, and PEC Zwolle. At Ajax, he scored the winning goal in the 1973 European Cup Final, against Juventus. At Bastia, he took the side to the UEFA Cup Final in 1978. At Saint-Etienne, he played with Michel Platini. So he brought a wealth of experience, and the free-flowing maverick was more measured and relaxed than Cruyff.

When he started out at Ajax, he played in the youth team and the second team, learning the Ajax way but he suffered in terms of his actual appearances – his breakthrough took a while as he would have to oust club legend Sjaak Swaart.

Rep was no pushover and still had that Dutch logicality when required, and like Cruyff he knew his mind. When playing for Valencia he despised the training techniques of their coach, the Paraguayan Heriberto Herrera. He disagreed with his approach, claiming there was too much discipline and running with no coaching. The team ran all day, but there was no work on technique, no football. The focus was on running and stamina. It got so bad that he had to leave. The Valencia board wouldn't allow him to, so Rep paid £150,000 of his own money to buy out his contract.

Rep had the experience to add to his undoubted skill and confidence. But this Feyenoord side needed some fresh legs and urgency, not another box office curiosity. Ajax won the title, PSV were second and Feyenoord finished the season in third place.

The one-time Dutch superstar would later be left penniless, turning to drink after two failed marriages. His life was chaotic and he found himself homeless, spending most of his life travelling around in a motor home, with some freelance work for Dutch newspaper *De Telegraaf*.

Following some unsuccessful spells in coaching, he was desperate and approached Ajax about being a scout for them but they rejected him. Football always looks after its own, doesn't it? This was shameful behaviour towards a man who won the European Cup for the club. He played in two World Cup finals and is arguably one of the nation's finest players but was discarded. That's the type of mindset behind people running football. Take a bow, blazers. Nice touch.

Chapter 27

The Next Chapter, Netherlands Demise and Coaching Badges

IMAGINE HOW this day would have felt. You are Johan Cruyff. You've concluded a season at Feyenoord, won the league and cup, even the sportswriters have voted you the best player in the nation. You have ended a long, stellar career which took you to Ajax, Barcelona, LA Aztecs, Washington Diplomats, Levante, back to Ajax, then Feyenoord. You've practically won every major trophy and award possible. You've starred at the World Cup and almost won the competition. You appeared 48 times for your country, scoring 33 goals. To find the appropriate superlatives only serves to highlight your inadequacies. But the day has come. It is over. The playing career has gone. While he was playing at his peak, full-on, for Barcelona and the Netherlands, he was either training, travelling or playing. There was little time for family and relaxation.

When his financial situation drastically changed, Cruyff was still good enough to come back to the game, realising he had quit too soon – and proved he was able to come back to play, missing only one game throughout a long season, aged 37. But here he was, the first day with no football. He had played for 20 years, then the following day it was over. Nowadays, lesser players would require therapy. The reality had set in. What was he going to do? To go from the intensity of the spotlight as one of the world's biggest football stars to a guy with nothing to do, it must have been challenging.

When Cruyff finished playing at Feyenoord, he had a year out of the game to recharge but of course, he was always watching football. It's amazing what you notice when you're not part of things and observing from a distance. When you are away from home for a while, and return, you only see faults and imperfections, those unimportant jobs you put off. Cruyff spotted many problems in the way the Netherlands national side were playing which urgently needed to be fixed.

By 1984, Cruyff's once-great national side were on the wane. The mighty Dutch hadn't qualified for the World Cup in Spain in 1982, nor the next European Championship and would miss out on the World Cup in 1986. Something was seriously wrong at the very heart of the Dutch game. After defeat in the 1978 World Cup Final against Argentina, Total Football or at least the positive attacking elements of the Dutch style, had been allowed to wither and die on the vine.

In hindsight, with the way he played and read the game, Cruyff may have been better placed having a Dutch TV show called *The Fixer*, going around clubs, having an overview, seeing where things were going wrong and fixing it, like a consultant role. The Dutch national side were plummeting down the world rankings and, worse still, their failures to qualify weren't being properly addressed in an urgent enough manner.

Cruyff, as a proud Dutchman, a football person and now a fan, could see the problem. There was a shortage of coaching expertise. There weren't enough people with the required skill who had played at an elite level and who could help improve the technical ability of the players. It wasn't rocket science, it was quite simple, and obvious, to him at least. He would see issues and small problems which, if not changed, would lead to serious issues. He could give clear and tangible examples. In one case, from his youth days at Ajax, his mentor Jany van der Veen, who had been a player, would teach and coach the kids not only with technical ability but insight and chat to them about how to play the game.

In bad weather, he would have to take the training inside, making use of a gym hall. The players would be unhappy but make do. Here, van der Veen, in Cruyff's words, would 'make a virtue out of necessity'. He would hang the net and split the team into two sides and the players had to head the ball over. They were taught drills and to jump and head the ball but to do it correctly. Cruyff once said, 'Later, I headed in the deciding second-half goal against Inter in the 1972 European Cup Final. It was executed with technical perfection. Even though someone my height shouldn't have been tall enough to make the header. All thanks to a rainy-day exercise that my youth team coach came up with on the spot.' Imagine how simple that sounds – being taught how to jump higher and to head a ball correctly.

For Cruyff this was the issue with the international team – the KNVB coaches lacked technical expertise, handed down by former players. Now the Dutch football authorities wanted their coaches to have a diploma. Cruyff blamed it squarely on the shoulders of the KNVB. It was madness. Everyone would be coached from a textbook. No experience, like Jany, telling kids or youth team players how to do one thing properly, technically, like jumping to head a ball.

For Cruyff's generation, football from textbooks meant there was no rough and tumble and no hard tackling. It was too friendly. Football was a game and you had to learn the skill, but you also had to be competitive. The Dutch used to be technically brilliant but now they weren't. That was the problem.

Cruyff's first job back in football, and one which would prove the first rung on the coaching ladder, would come in 1985. He had been approached by the owners of Roda JC Kerkrade to come on board as an adviser. Then, MVV Maastricht, who had invited a successful sports businessman to help restructure their club, approached Cruyff to organise their youth setup. He was slowly coming back into football and his coaching journey had begun. Nothing would have football directors and presidents twitching more than seeing someone of Cruyff's skill and stature coming back into the game, and soon both Feyenoord and Ajax made offers to him.

It may not have felt like it at the time but Cruyff's arrival at Ajax, for his second playing spell in 1981, was the unofficial start of his coaching career. In his first game after returning from America, aged 34, he put in an imperious performance against Haarlem. He scored with a magnificent lob shot over the keeper, sending the place wild, and set up another in a 4-1 victory.

While playing, he worked with Frank Rijkaard, Marco van Basten, John Bosman, Sonny Silooy and John van't Schip. He revolutionised their game and method of play. Cruyff was a natural coach. He told team-mates what to do, whether they wanted to hear it or not. Ajax's three Danes, Søren Lerby, Jesper Olsen and from 1982, Jan Molby, took the concept and heavily influenced Denmark's style of play, to widespread praise in the Mexico World Cup of 1986.

Again, when you look back at his performances during his year in Rotterdam, one thing is obvious – he is controlling and taking over the game. He was a player-coach in the final season at Feyenoord. He had already started the next sensational stage of his footballing legacy. As an older member of the team, you had Cruyff helping groups of players at both Ajax and Feyenoord who would go on to star at the highest level.

By 1985, Cruyff was refreshed, reinvigorated and the time was right for both parties. Ajax were Cruyff's club. They were keen to forget the recent past and despite claiming he would not do anything in rancour or for revenge, Cruyff admitted he had buried the hatchet. Love was in the air. He was eventually appointed as Ajax's technical director in June 1985 but not before the appliance of some dark arts, straight out of a political thriller.

There was some strategic manoeuvring, canvassing and dirty work to be done to get to this point and Cruyff wasn't subtle about how he'd make it happen. Dennis Bergkamp explained in his book, *Stillness and Speed: My Story*, 'Restless, he was soon looking for a way into management preferably with Ajax. The only club in Holland he cared about. That the club already had a rather good coach, Aad de Mos, the chairman hated him and Cruyff didn't have a coaching badge [as Dutch FA rules believed he must] were the merest of difficulties.'

To smooth the path to Cruyff's appointment Aad de Mos had begun to be undermined by players, particularly Cruyff's closest allies in the side, van Basten and van't Schip, culminating in his eventual sacking. Chairman Harmsen had finally given in to peer and media pressure and the clamour for Cruyff to be appointed. The lingering issue was, however, how to allow Cruyff to coach without his badges. This would be solved by describing him as a 'technical director', not a coach. Cruyff had taken three disadvantages and turned them into an advantage. No matter the method behind gaining control, an unsavoury form of bloodletting Cruyff himself was subject to as a player, his impact as 'technical director' would be immediate.

It's a common title now, but it was the first time it had been used in Dutch football. Cruyff readily admitted and enjoyed reminding people, especially the KNVB, that it was a loophole to allow him to manage without having to get his football diploma and badges. He was now manager of Ajax.

It always came back to the friction between Cruyff and the country's governing body, and that clash of two cultures. The Dutch football authorities had embarked upon a development programme allowing people to become qualified coaches. If you wanted to coach or referee in the Netherlands, you had to have completed the course, earned the diploma and have a certificate to say so. It's commonplace in football associations around the world.

On the other side you had the polar opposite. The idea of a football manual and a diploma scares and shocks a maverick player like Cruyff. It insults his intelligence. To him, football is far too intuitive to learn from textbooks. The KNVB said no, it was part of its core values and strategy, from grassroots to elite coaching. Both sides become embittered, ingrained and entrenched and Cruyff more so than most. His attitude was to recoil from anything that stifles creativity and independent thought.

You can understand the KNVB's approach of having an educational system set in place, hoping to improve the game. But then you are asking one of the best players the country has ever created, who has a football move named after him, who is credited with popularising and advancing Total Football, to sit a test so he can work in football? It's like asking Einstein to take his teachers' training to teach science.

What Cruyff may have been rallying against wasn't the exam itself but the type of people running football – the administrators, the football civil servants the game seems to universally attract. Those small-minded, pernickety, tie and blazer mentality types, exist in every country. They give the impression they are people who enjoy holding a grudge.

In Scotland, the blazers used to run the game like a golf club. It was a sport heavily governed by pernickety and, to most sane people unimportant rules and regulations, a narrow-minded view of anything which didn't conform. Scotland, at one point, invited Rinus Michels over to set up a think tank, so maybe that's where the connection was made. It beggars belief that one of the greatest players of his generation would need to have his coaching badges and a diploma before he could coach. There appeared to be two distinct camps: those determined to keep Cruyff in his place, as no one is bigger than the game; and those who believe genius can't be and shouldn't be tamed. Over time though, it would have proven easier if he had sat his exams to become a KNVB coach.

The issue rumbled on. We are talking about Cruyff here, and we have learned he was not short of self-belief and belligerent to the end. Equally, he knew how to apply pressure to get his way, or at least force others to have a re-think. He decided, along with Michels, that he would write to the KNVB – Michels was the technical director – in a veiled attempt at having the rules changed. He suggested that those who had played both at club and international level should have the chance to take the exam first and receive tuition on the parts they failed. This would speed up the process of fast-tracking experienced players with technical knowledge into positions where they could improve the game.

Cruyff believed his actions were not just for his benefit but would help the national game too. The more players who had played at an elite level who became coaches, within the KNVB infrastructure, the better the chance of improvement for the national side.

Cruyff later admitted he would have struggled with parts of the exam, because of the way he distilled and understood the game: 'In doing this, I was taking a big personal risk. In practical terms, I would have breezed through subjects like tactics and technique but because I thought in such a different way about football than most people, and certainly in a different way from the people running the course, I'd have probably never have made it through the exam.'

In the end, it wouldn't matter. As time passed by, Cruyff would not hear back from the KNVB. It was implied that the organisation would discuss the points raised in his letter but nothing came of it. Those in charge at Ajax came up with the title of technical director and Cruyff would officially launch his coaching career. If he had a bit more belief in himself – yes even the indefatigable Cruyff was nervous with exams – and completed the course, he would've been fine I'm sure. It may have helped him later when the national job came up.

This was 1985, though, and Cruyff was back at his beloved Ajax. Surprisingly, everything in the garden was rosy and his world was serene, for now.

Chapter 28

Johan Cruyff Technical Director

AS AJAX coach, Cruyff immediately re-established the philosophy of Total Football. He also added his grace notes and tweaks. The youth system was overhauled, and every team educated in the way of Total Football; uniformity throughout the club, playing the same way from the under-eight side to the first team.

Now his project was in motion. Under Rinus Michels, he had learned about discipline and technique. With Jany van der Veen and Vic Buckingham, he had been guided and brought up with the values of Ajax. Now as coach he was ready. It was time to launch his football revolution.

These principles would eventually be factored out and filter through not only Ajax but the rest of Dutch football and the national side. He would later do the same on a bigger, more complex scale, at Barcelona, and from there the Spanish national team would also find huge success, playing football the way Cruyff wanted it played: creatively, in a sophisticated style. This started when he became Ajax coach.

He established ground rules and some ideas people would find difficult to process. Winning and glory would initially be less important than the way each team performed. But if they did that correctly and got it right, they would eventually win games anyway. Cruyff revolutionised football not only through technique, talent and discipline and his desire to attack and play Total Football but also his arrogance, fractiousness and sheer will to dominate situations on and off the pitch.

When he started coaching at Ajax, the KNVB and the trainers' association were soon visiting, watching and asking why he was training the players. Cruyff suggested due to his elite training schedule as a player, he had to keep fit.

While in the US, he had learned about the emphasis on specialist training. He utilised three assistants: Cor van der Hart, a defensive coach; the delightfully named Spitz Kohn, a striker and attacking coach; and Tonny Bruins Slot, who was Ajax's chief scout and a highly valued and experienced coach. He would be Cruyff's assistant at Ajax, leaving with him to work in Barcelona. Cruyff also brought in a fitness coach and was the first in Dutch football to bring in a goalkeeping coach, whose brief was to focus on coaching every goalkeeper at the club from the first team down. It was quite refreshing and innovative then, but now it's commonplace.

In total there were seven technical staff helping improve the technique of the players, plus a scouting network. Cruyff's role, apart from overseeing the development, was to hone and improve the finer details. It was a huge leap of faith for the players and coaching staff and required a root and branch overhaul for the club. Cruyff left his staff to do their specific job, in their area of expertise, trusting them to get on with it.

When he got to work, his ideas started to click. Cruyff realised the brand, the Total Football style the Netherlands had successfully played, had been allowed to drift. The intensity and tempo of training were upped. There was also a change of culture as coaches were actively encouraged to pass on and share their knowledge in an environment of continuous improvement. On the pitch they wanted to entertain and attack with three strikers, a player behind them, a goalkeeper playing out of the box and a centre-half pushing forward into the inside-left position. It was like Ajax circa the 1970s already.

Cruyff's philosophy was about positional fluidity. Passing forward and attacking were the only criteria. Pundits wondered what the formation was – 3-5-2 perhaps, or maybe a 4-3-3? Most would've found themselves counting the number of players Ajax had on the pitch. His team shape was also the same – a sweeper-keeper, three mobile defenders with one covering space as a de facto defensive midfielder. Two controlling midfielders fed the attacking midfielders, and further ahead were a second striker, two touchline-hugging wingers and a versatile centre-forward. The same shape was used by Rinus Michels.

When Koeman and Vanenburg left Ajax to sign for PSV, Cruyff replaced them with hardened, tough professionals in Jan Wouters and Danny Blind. If Wouters and Blind were the steel then left-footed Arnold Mühren, bought from Manchester United, was the silk. They even had their sweeper-keeper in Stanley Menzo who behaved like a hyperactive jack-in-the-box, such was his aversion to staying on his line.

Cruyff would go on to win a trophy every year he was in charge at Ajax. The KNVB Cup came in the first year, giving them qualification to the European Cup Winners' Cup, which they won the following year, with the youngest ever team. It is not easy to win a major European trophy and they faced difficult opposition in Bursaspor, Olympiacos, Malmö and Real Zaragoza before meeting Lokomotive Leipzig in the final in Athens. Clearly, he was doing something right. In a bizarre turnaround, after this victory, the KNVB had a blazer amnesty, forgave the idea of Cruyff being a 'technical director' and awarded him an honorary coaching diploma.

As well as focusing on the technical aspects of the game while in the US, Cruyff also learned how a modern professional sports business should be operated and noticed how badly Ajax was run. The Amsterdam club had allowed itself to stagnate. There was already friction between the coach and the board. For Cruyff, the club's philosophy was more important. The board didn't care about his philosophy, they wanted to win. For Cruyff, it was always about *how* are you going to win? If Ajax played his way, they would win everything anyway. Cruyff spoke out at their short-term thinking, making himself unpopular. But he believed in a way of developing Ajax, and those running it didn't share his vision. When it came to transfers the club were too slow to move for an available player; they weren't investing in players and sold their best ones too cheaply.

In 1987, Marco van Basten signed for Silvio Berlusconi's AC Milan for £1.5m. For that price, the Italians had signed a player who had scored the winning goal in a major European final. He had netted 138 goals in 145 games for Ajax and in his penultimate campaign he had notched 37 league goals in just 26 matches. Cheap at half the price, but the Ajax business model was out of touch.

We know Cruyff wasn't perfect. No one that brilliant is. We also know football is driven by ego, with directors, chairmen and owners who can't stay out of the limelight and interfere, who think it's their success when it's going well and can't be found when it goes wrong. For the project to work, Cruyff needed a patient, rich, benefactor who agreed whole-heartedly with everything he suggested or did. That person needed to understand how football worked and accept the time required for evolution, and for results to improve. That's fantasy football.

Cruyff had demonstrated he could build a side in his image and make them aware of their duty to entertain. His Ajax team performed superbly with Rijkaard, van't Schip, Koeman and van Basten exceptional, scoring 127 goals, though PSV would win the league. At Ajax, between 1985 and 1988, Cruyff would successfully coach a youthful group to win the European Cup Winners' Cup and two KNVB Cup wins. But Ajax wouldn't spend. They were content to play it safe, and to win titles Cruyff knew he needed better players. For Cruyff, the only issue now was to find a club big enough to match his ambitions. They hailed from Catalonia and played in the Nou Camp.

Chapter 29

Homage to Catalonia
Part 2: The *efecto mariposa*

JOINING BARCELONA in the summer of 1988, Cruyff had some major work to do. He had the uncanny skill – he did the same at Ajax – of delivering silverware to keep fans and his board happy while trying to build a side that could win the league and the European Cup. In 1989 he won the European Cup Winners' Cup and in 1990 the Copa del Rey.

It would take until 1990/91 before his team had the correct blend, finally playing the style of football at the level he required. Cruyff had to be shrewd as transfers were restricted and he could only sign three foreigners. He had Hristo Stoichkov, Michael Laudrup and Ronald Koeman. Bulgarian Stoichkov was one of Cruyff's favourites as not only could he play, he had the required mental toughness and tenacity.

It was Cruyff, aged 43, who had to be tenacious for the time being. He had acute stomach pains, was vomiting and had a fever. Something wasn't right. His wife begged him to be checked out, then thankfully dragged him to a doctor. In a three-hour operation, he underwent double heart bypass surgery.

After his operation, Cruyff would return within four weeks. His consultant praised his positive and upbeat mental attitude, claiming, rather surprisingly, that he was an excellent patient. Later, however, Cruyff would admit to loving watching surgery and would be present with any players going through operations, learning and watching and becoming something of a medical expert.

Carles Rexach, his assistant manager, got Cruyff's first LaLiga title over the line. The side would also reach the 1991 European Cup Winners' Cup Final, losing 2-1 to Manchester United in De Kuip, Rotterdam, a stadium familiar to Cruyff. But the following year would become one of the most memorable in the club's recent history.

From Cruyff's arrival in 1988, the Nou Camp was bouncing and crowds once lower than 40,000 were over 80,000. Cruyff and the Barca fans were happy. They started to win, claiming the first of four consecutive titles and then the European Cup. The Dream Team had finally come together. But it took time. 'To be able to play like that', said Cruyff, 'you need to be fast, and you have to keep on switching gear. It took more than 10,000 hours of training to finally reach the level of the Dream Team.'

Diehard Barcelona fans believe Cruyff's time as coach with the Dream Team is the best football in the club's modern era. When he arrived from Ajax in 1973, as a player, Barcelona were toiling in the league. Cruyff would turn things around. When he became manager in 1988, Barcelona was a club on its knees, hobbling from disaster to crisis, underperforming, debt-ridden and the unthinkable had started to happen; even their fans had grown frustrated with them.

Cruyff's 'second coming' gave the club hope and an identity, and his disciples followed. His personality, and crucially, his style of play, was coming together. The people had a cause again, something worth fighting for and believing in. The better the team became, the more it fed into Catalan politics.

When fascist dictator Franco rose to power in the late 1930s, he set about suppressing republicanism. He had forbidden people to speak in Catalan. Both the Catalans and the Basques wanted independence and were targeted. Even Barca had to change their name to the more Spanish, 'Club futbol Barcelona'.

Cruyff grew up in the 1960s, amid the counter culture of liberal Amsterdam. He was someone who believed in expression and did express himself, on and off the pitch. Originally, as a player, he had, whether he wanted to or not, become a lightning rod for positive change. He immediately got Barca's mantra of 'Més que un club'. They were more than just a club, they were a cause. He loved the passion of the Catalans and would eventually manage the Catalan national side. As a player, he won the title, beat Real Madrid 5-0 in the Bernabéu, and when he kissed his Catalan captain's armband after being sent off, he won the hearts and minds of the people.

Throughout his career, Cruyff tended to have his favourite players he could see something of himself in, or at least those who understood the game and how it should be played. Pep Guardiola and Dennis Bergkamp are two great examples. Guardiola was the same and could read the game; intelligent, a great communicator on and off the field of play. When Pep was coming through, Cruyff believed he had talent when many didn't. Critics rounded on Guardiola and the club wanted to let him go. They thought he was a hopeless defender who couldn't run or head the ball. Cruyff looked at him differently, realising he could coach and work on his weaknesses. He could see Pep knew how to do the instinctive things like read the game, had football intelligence and insight and those were impossible to teach.

He was unafraid to take a chance on a promising youth player. Guardiola spoke extensively in a wonderful interview to *The Guardian*'s Donald McRae, before the official launch of Cruyff's autobiography. It's worth seeking out online, such was its quality and sense of capturing a normally guarded Guardiola. Perhaps Pep was emotional, or nervous ahead of speaking at the book launch but like a great journalist should, Donald McRae perfectly captured the mood.

Guardiola explained that Cruyff was brave with any youth team players with promise, 'He was the most courageous coach and manager I ever met. When he smells the talent it doesn't matter if the age is 16 or 17 because he believed in, what in Spain we call, the *efecto mariposa* [the butterfly effect]. For him, one good pass at the beginning could create absolutely everything.' Guardiola's admiration for his former boss, mentor and friend was evident when he told McRae, 'He was the most influential person in football history. He changed not one club. He changed two clubs as a player and a coach.'

Like most football coaches, Guardiola speaks in glowing terms of his mentor, as Cruyff would about Rinus Michels, but you can tell these aren't glib asides or some comfortable after-dinner circuit anecdotes about the lads, and the dressing room. These are the heartfelt words of a man who feels lucky and blessed, like a son reminiscing about his father. It's an emotional intensity, driven by a shared passion for a sport they love. There is gratitude and modesty: 'I knew nothing about football before knowing Cruyff. He was unique, totally unique. Without him, I wouldn't be here. I know for sure this is why I am, right now the manager of Manchester City and before that Bayern Munich and Barcelona.'

Guardiola emotionally and eloquently described Cruyff's significance and importance in the history of Barcelona, 'Before he came we didn't have a cathedral of football, this beautiful church, at Barcelona. We needed something new. And now it is something that has lasted. It was built by one man, by Johan Cruyff, stone by stone. That's why he was special.'

Cruyff, even as a coach, would come on to the training pitch and explain what he wanted. Even after he had retired, he was still able to play. 'He was better than us,' Guardiola says of the side who won Barcelona's first European Cup in 1992. 'He was much, much better than us. He explained what we have to do and showed us how to do it. It was a masterclass every single training session, every single game, analysing why we played good or bad. It was like going to university every day.'

When Cruyff became honorary president of Barcelona in April 2010 and was interviewed by Barca TV he was pushed about the importance of systems and how Guardiola and Rijkaard had updated the club's way of playing. Cruyff seemed to modestly debunk the starry-eyed fixation of Total Football and his philosophy. Guardiola claimed systems were only a starting point; in other words, the way you played meant nothing if you didn't have the players to execute it. Cruyff was somewhat pragmatic, confirming it was about possession, distance and players, 'You always have to be flexible and not have any fixed ideas. The system is not so important. You need to have capable, technically good players to understand how things should be done.'

Cruyff considered for a second before clarifying, 'With Romário, during my time as coach, you played one system, but when Laudrup played there it was a different system. But both were central strikers. It is all about distances and how far apart the players are. It will never be a risky thing because if you have possession of the ball then there is no problem.' Systems were only workable if you had the players to implement them. You couldn't do anything if you didn't have possession of the ball.

Romário was an interesting case study. He was an incredible player, one of those who got you a goal when one was desperately needed. Barca fans loved him and he gave the impression that he wasn't doing enough, then he would pop up and show his brilliance in the box and get the winner. His time at the club was underpinned by a feeling he conserved his energy or his 'goalscoring luck' for the 1994 World Cup. He liked to party, and during his time in Barcelona he lived in a hotel. The player infuriated and frustrated many, but Cruyff got the best out of him. Yet the late Sir Bobby Robson had a more insightful opinion, 'He was an exciting player, who was capable of turning a game in an instant ... but he could also be frustrating, disappearing for long periods of the game, rarely shouldering any responsibility and sometimes socialising and dancing late into the night before important games.'

Cruyff's coaching career, arguably, equalled and possibly eclipsed his magnificent playing career. As a player, the medals, trophies, and awards he won far outweighed those as a coach but his biggest achievement as a manager was the far-reaching way his footballing philosophy was embraced and adopted around the world. He would love the medals and titles but football being played with elegance and treated as entertainment was paramount.

He also loved the idea of finding, nurturing and developing players like Marco van Basten and Dennis Bergkamp. Coaching some of the best players of their generation would be worth more than a medal or tin cup. His persistence in attaining perfection and demanding the best would come at a price. But it proved worthwhile. If he hadn't existed, football would most likely look like another sport.

When Barcelona won the European Cup, the city came to a standstill. There were celebrations and parties as the Catalan people displayed their jubilance at finally winning the biggest prize. It is unbelievable to consider that it took until 1992 for a club with their fan base and size to take the trophy. They would make up for lost time in the following two decades.

After the victory, the players stood on the balcony of City Hall. Waving, with the trophy gleaming beside him, Cruyff was invited to the microphone. He looked every bit like the president. And, on that night, if they had a snap election, he would've been voted in by a landslide. 'En un memento dado ('at one point' – a funny reference to Cruyff's favourite, oft-repeated expression). Now we've won the first one, the second one is coming.'

Txiki Begiristain, Manchester City's director of football since 2012, played on the left wing for Cruyff in the Dream Team. He is credited, when at Barcelona under both Rijkaard and Guardiola, with applying the same principles as Cruyff to his recruitment and player development. Reflecting after Cruyff's death, Begiristain said that one often overlooked aspect of his personality was his bravery. He was, unlike his players, fearless, 'When there are doubts, people tend to seek safety in numbers, to go with the herd. Not Cruyff. His first solution was always to be more attacking, more expansive. Three at the back and the centre-back is Ronald Koeman? Instead of full-backs, midfielders? Every time he sought a solution, he attacked more. And when he told us what he was doing, we thought, "Is he mad or what?"'

If Cruyff were alive today he'd be grateful that one of his players recognised his courage but would be most proud of the fact his methodology and a particular way of playing the beautiful game was accepted as the standard across the globe. Cruyff had delivered as a coach at Barcelona but had started a second phase when he decided to break down his Dream Team and build a new one, which takes time. Football is about evolution not revolution as the great teams who brought success originally grow old, become jaded, or need to be replaced.

It took the club three years to pay homage to Cruyff. The testimonial game held in 1999 proved to be a special evening. Children, mums, dads, grandparents and the hardcore fans created an unusual atmosphere more like an outdoor mass as all came to say thank you. Cruyff looked out and the fans had already packed out the ground 45 minutes before the game began. The noise was something else, with banners everywhere, and the supporters were rejoicing. It was a friendly between the current side, managed by Louis van Gaal, and the famous Dream Team, which starred Hristo Stoichkov, Brian Laudrup and Ronald Koeman. The score didn't matter, although it finished 2-0 to van Gaal's men.

In August 2020, Barcelona revealed a statue of Hendrik Johannes Cruijff. It is located at the entrance of the Nou Camp, at the grandstand. The 3.5-metre bronze figure by Dutch sculptress Corry Ammerlaan van Niekerk is unusual for a modern creation – it actually looks like the subject. Better still, it perfectly captures his spirit. Cruyff is at his peak, playing for Barcelona, characteristically pointing and instructing and telling team-mates where they need to move to.

The statue was unveiled within days of the club going through one of their biggest institutional crises in decades. Barcelona had endured humiliation at the hands of Bayern Munich in the Champions League semi-final. They were embarrassed, slaughtered and disgraced in an 8-2 defeat. Coach Quique Setién was sacked after the inept and lifeless display.

Ronald Koeman was appointed and quickly underlined he would show the door to anyone showing lack of commitment. Rumours swirled around that Piqué, Busquets, Messi and Suárez could be on their way out as Koeman felt teams winning the Champions League showed more athleticism and aggression, which was lacking in some of the current squad. Messi set the internet ablaze and Twitter into meltdown by expressing that he wanted to leave the club. The talk was that he would team up with former boss Pep Guardiola at Manchester City. Barcelona were in the middle of an existential crisis. Those present must have been wishing Johan could come to life and help guide the club through this stormy time.

Cruyff's move to coach Barcelona is now regarded as a significant turning point and a watershed moment. The full extent of the changes he made, and the people he put in place and mentored, with a focus on the youth academy and a way of playing, saw a sea change in the club's fortunes. Before 1990, they had won only ten titles since their formation. Up to 2020 they had secured 16 league titles and won the European Cup/ Champions League five times.

Chapter 30

The *De Telegraaf* Column

ONE OF the saddest parts of Johan Cruyff's passing in 2016 was that he did not live to see the radical changes he had put in place come to fruition. By 2017, Ajax began to turn around as a direct result of changes made to the youth system which would see a return to Total Football.

By 2018/19, when Ajax played Tottenham Hotspur in the semi-final of the Champions League, six of their players had come via the academy and Jong Ajax systems. These players would have benefited from the changes Cruyff implemented. If it wasn't his side, it was one that evolved thanks to the processes and changes he made which helped deliver it.

Erik ten Hag was a disciple of and worked for Pep Guardiola at Bayern Munich before becoming Ajax coach and instilling Cruyff's methods into the team. The young group were seconds away from reaching the final but were defeated by a late Lucas Moura goal. And, as before, Ajax would sell off their talent to the major European superpowers like Barcelona and Juventus. Ajax were, in football terms, technically and financially, now in great shape.

With a career as player and coach picking fights and finding fault with those running the game, it was hardly surprising – in hindsight, it seems unforgivable – but Cruyff from 1996 never managed at the top level again. From November 2009 to January 2013, he coached the Catalan national side managing friendly games against Argentina, Honduras, Tunisia and Nigeria. It is not affiliated to FIFA or UEFA so not allowed to participate in the World Cup or the European Championship. He kept busy with his Cruyff Foundation and media commitments.

As well as being a great TV pundit, Cruyff had a hard-hitting column in *De Telegraaf,* where each week, he let rip at the state of the game. As much as the football world would have preferred to see him coaching, or in some kind of technical or general manager role, the outlet was great for him. Controversial, opinionated, unafraid to upset people, he was the perfect columnist. In one particular piece, in September 2010 after Ajax's 2-0 defeat in the Champions League against Real Madrid at the Bernabéu, he took no prisoners.

Cruyff's column had a profound impact. At this point, he must have felt like Michael Corleone in *The Godfather Part III,* when he is relentlessly hectored to return to sort the family business when he knows he should be shuffling off into a more respectable and peaceful life, with the immortal line, 'Just when I thought I was out, they pull me back in.'

In Cruyff's column, he was extremely critical toward those running the club and angered at the performance, more the nature of the defeat. He used his platform in the country's biggest-selling newspaper to tell the nation, 'This Is No Longer Ajax'. Cruyff stated that the team on show was even worse than the one Rinus Michels inherited at the inception of his revolution in 1965. The technique wasn't there, and more alarmingly, the football basics weren't there. The philosophy is simple: when you have possession, make the pitch big. When you don't, make it small again. Cruyff was angry as it was rudimentary, something kids used to be taught from the moment they arrived at Ajax. There was a lack of football knowledge at every level. They were also missing former players to coach and pass on advice. He was dismayed by what he witnessed, and in the way Ajax were beaten by Real Madrid.

For him, the game, the style of play, Total Football, was above everything and everyone. It was an obsession and people must understand that playing football in this entertaining, pulsating, clever manner was the only way to do it. It took precedence over everything he did as a player, coach and technical director. Cruyff turned on his country after watching the World Cup Final in 2010. The Dutch faced Spain and played what he called 'anti-football' and he launched a scathing attack on coach Bert van Marwijk's side. On 12 July 2010, he told BBC Sport, 'This ugly, vulgar, hard, hermetic, hardly eye-catching, hardly football style, yes it served the Dutch to unsettle Spain. If with this they got satisfaction, fine, but they ended up losing. They were playing anti-football.' Cruyff also managed to criticise match referee Howard Webb, too.

Despite his many flaws, Cruyff still believed in talent and was old-school, believing knowledge should be passed on and shared. It had to be handed down. He reached out and encouraged those he felt had something about their personality, communications skills or intelligence which hinted at a career in coaching. He might have expected more of his disciples to succeed in management, especially Dennis Bergkamp and Marco van Basten. Frank Rijkaard did well at Barcelona but it was Bergkamp who seemed primed to step up. He has since stated, quite categorically, that he wouldn't become a coach but he was convinced by Cruyff in 2011/12 to take on a role as assistant manager and striker coach for Frank de Boer. When Peter Bosz arrived at Ajax in 2016, Bergkamp seemed happy to take a back seat, coaching youth players and preparing them for life in the first team. But maybe there's something in his nature that isn't quite ferocious enough, as he admits he would prefer to be in charge of an academy as part of a team but not the boss.

In December 2017, Bergkamp was sacked after a coaching reshuffle made by Ajax's general manager, Edwin van der Sar and technical director Marc Overmars. Despite Bergkamp's sacking, Cruyff said, 'They will accuse me of short-sightedness, but if I think about a guitarist, I see Keith Richards; if I think about a painter, Johannes Vermeer. But if someone were to wake me up and ask me "footballer", I tend to see Dennis Bergkamp. He looks like a footballer to me.'

The aftermath of the *De Telegraaf* column had a profound effect – but not an entirely positive one. Cruyff stuck by his words, and soon a chain of events would lead to major change. He wrote, 'If you looked at who represented the club, you immediately saw that there was a lack of football knowledge there. There wasn't a single first-team player on the commissioners' council, the board, the members' council or the club administration. Not one! So it wasn't surprising the club was failing to play decent football – the administrators didn't have the first clue about tactics and techniques that the club had been built on.' In other words, a philosophy built on technically gifted players playing attacking football.

Things started to turn ugly. Cruyff suggested that Ajax fans come together and nominate new candidates for the upcoming council elections. Then the fans could vote in ex-players able to improve technical expertise throughout each team at every age group of the youth system. It escalated into a huge story in Dutch football, eventually ending up in court. It became known as the 'Velvet Revolution', but it was a dirty fight and would lead to further acrimony between Cruyff and van Gaal. Sponsors left the club and the directors needed police protection from fans. For many, it was a price worth paying to win back the soul of the club and resetting Ajax on its traditional path.

Cruyff was hurt seeing his club destroyed but the bigger picture was how far off course Ajax had been allowed to drift from everything it once stood for. He wanted to restructure the youth system, from the under-sevens to the under-18s, and have a coach treating each group accordingly. For instance, the needs of a child understanding how to run into space, to tackle and pass were poles apart from the needs of a player who needed to be prepared, coached and advised on coping with the pressure of playing in the first team. This would eventually become known as the 'Cruyff Plan'. It was an attempt to instil the once respected and highly regarded traditions of Ajax.

At the heart of it lay an attack on the suits running the club, and how far they had allowed the standards to slip from those core values. Those coaching at each age group, in his opinion, were not accomplished enough, technically. After a few false starts and the usual fall-outs, and 'professional differences of opinion' Cruyff eventually joined the board of commissioners in February 2011 as an adviser, and would be part of a technical advisory group, one of the three sounding boards to advise on technical issues.

Before this, Cruyff had reached out to former Ajax legends and two coaches then employed at the club, Wim Jonk and Ruben Jongkind. In an interview, speaking about the plan, Jongkind explained to Sky Sports journalist Adam Bate that they were invited to a secret meeting in a house in Amsterdam. The latter brought paper, a pen and had a plan. 'We were invited there. I was not a former player so I'm at this secret meeting with these guys,' said Jongkind, 'and it was like, woah, s***. The former players had made an analysis but did not have solutions. Wim Jonk and I had written down a plan, a way you should reorganise the academy and some other ways to improve the club.'

From the club's point of view, if you sat on the board, why would you roll over? They accused Cruyff of making ridiculous demands and playing to the crowd. Ajax's general director Rik van den Boog and chairman Uri Coronel refused to play ball. They even suggested that Cruyff was out of touch with how modern clubs operated. Football was run through governance not grandstanding through a newspaper column.

When Cruyff thought he had made inroads, he always ended up down a one-way street. This wasn't football, it was politics, people with no interest or knowledge of the game looking after themselves. Something didn't ring true though. He would be undermined when the board deliberately appointed Louis van Gaal as general manager, without asking Cruyff's opinion.

In 2011, the Cruyff Plan, executed by his guys – Dennis Bergkamp, Wim Jonk, and Ruben Jongkind – was up and running. This was football though, and the two biggest problems Cruyff faced were self-preservation and fear of change. Football and big business find it difficult to implement change quickly. You have idealism versus pragmatism. It's remarkably easy for organisations and businesses to slow the process down. They refuse to accept change, question every suggestion and are reluctant to embrace anything innovative.

Cruyff's plan would only work if the details were uniformly followed by everyone in the process. Jonk would oversee a bespoke coaching approach where each player would be treated individually, and the ambitious aim was to ensure three from each year could reach the first team. The method was to think of each player, not each team, and every single one of them had an individual development plan.

At the Ajax Academy, coaches would be responsible for individual players and not teams. The coaches would be changed to new teams on an eight-week rota. Cruyff applied his Total Football principles to how football should be coached.

Ruben Jongkind explained to Adam Bate how the plan worked. There was one playing style throughout the entire academy, 'Before this, it was as though every coach was his own island. They had some idea, of course, of Ajax. It was all different shades of the same colour. It was still the Ajax DNA but some coaches were not playing the football that we wanted to play.'

Again, it was back to Cruyff's principles: learning was more important than winning. 'We did not want the results to be important,' continued Jongkind. 'There is only one team that needs to win and that is the first team. A youth game is the same as training. It is a means to an end, not an end in itself. It is a tool.'

The club tried to sack Jonk from his position as head of the academy. He was the last general of the Cruyff Plan. He would not leave his post and was backed by his coaches in the youth system. Jonk held firm, believing and insisting the board weren't implementing the main aspects of the Cruyff plan either in the first team or in overall club policy. The mayhem though became too much for Cruyff, who decided he would no longer advise the club.

By December 2015, Cruyff was ill, and with Jonk eventually leaving because of 'irreconcilable differences', Cruyff soon followed along with 14 other coaches. The politics and in-fighting had become too much for him and, again, he used his column to announce that he'd had enough.

'I quit,' he wrote in *De Telegraaf*. 'For years, I have noticed that the core of my vision within Ajax hasn't been followed up. This feels like a raw deal. I'm just a director and I had high hopes the whole thing would be in good hands with a few experienced drivers. Those in charge at Ajax must sit together and look first at themselves. Make sure it will be fine, but it will not happen under the umbrella of the Cruyff Plan, because my name will not be there anymore.'

He was ill when he wrote this, having been diagnosed with lung cancer, and upset; he would die a few months later. He was frustrated but shouldn't have been as the changes he suggested, even the amended version, helped the club improve. The anger and frustration directed towards Ajax, which had been the starting point for the column, saw a course of action that in time, developed technical coaches preparing stars like Matthijs De Ligt, Donny van de Beek and to a lesser extent, Frenkie de Jong. Each was a wonderfully gifted technical player and starred for the Ajax first team before being sold on.

Older Cruyff fans would have raised a glass and had a rueful smile when Ajax beat Real Madrid over two legs in the 2018/19 Champions League. Down 2-1 from the first leg, they were written off but didn't just win, they destroyed Real Madrid 4-1 in the Bernabéu. It was an unbelievable result in a game which every football purist agreed was, on paper, a classic European match-up.

The victory set up a mouth-watering quarter-final against Juventus. The Amsterdammers were written off after the first leg thanks to Cristiano Ronaldo scoring the crucial away goal to make it 1-1. Erik ten Hag's men arrived in Turin to an over-confident media and defeated Juventus 2-1, going through on aggregate. They reached their first Champions League semi-final since 1997 and were seconds from the final only to suffer that heartbreaking defeat to Tottenham Hotspur. The results against Real Madrid and Juventus announced to the world that Ajax were back, playing spectacularly, and displaying a familiar brand of football.

Ten Hag made no bones about it. His side played to the same system and style as Cruyff's and then Pep Guardiola's, not only at Manchester City but Barcelona and Bayern Munich. He was unapologetic, 'Guardiola's philosophy is sensational and he has demonstrated this at Barcelona, Bayern and City. His structured, attacking play, is very attractive and I aim to implement this at Ajax.' So we have ten Hag unashamedly coaching a style of football at Ajax, gained from working with Guardiola, who learned from Cruyff. There is a perfect symmetry here.

Ten Hag's version of Total Football is even more robust. High-pressing full-backs play as attackers, wingers cut inside like midfielders, and Dušan Tadić has a free role directly behind the strikers. Frenkie de Jong – who maybe took the Cruyff template too far by also leaving Ajax to sign for Barcelona – is the classic product of the Cruyff/Guardiola/ten Hag prototype; a defensive, box-to-box midfielder, and playmaker. Of de Jong and Cruyff, long-time coach and friend Tonny Bruins Slot told *De Telegraaf*, 'Cruyff loved that style: the perception, the vision of play and going past two or three players dribbling. Cruyff's favourite players, like Faas Wilkes, his idol when he was younger, had those qualities.'

Ten Hag was part of Guardiola's coaching team at Bayern Munich, managing the reserve side before stepping into the top job at Ajax to replace Marcel Keizer in 2017. He is a huge admirer of Guardiola, especially the way he has adapted his style at Manchester City to suit the robust and fast English Premier League, 'Pep realised you can't play the kind of football he loves without having a couple of physically strong athletes – and so he brought them in. Yes, he is stubborn in his philosophy, but not in the execution. And that makes him the best. Guardiola only wants to win games with beautiful football, just like his teacher Johan Cruyff and has adapted to the culture in every country.'

As well as a shared approach tactically, they both share the belief that football should be played in a certain way. It had to be attacking and with flair. Ten Hag stated the case quite categorically in his press conference before the Real Madrid tie, 'Guardiola is an innovator and inspiration, he had great players at Barcelona, like Andres Iniesta, Lionel Messi, Xavi and others. But it takes a lot of quality from a coach to make top players play in a great way as a team. Everyone has to contribute. The team comes first and not the individual. Even Messi was more of a team player under Guardiola. He has never been as brilliant again as he was under Pep.'

So here we have a mutual appreciation society, bonded from one man – Johan Cruyff. Both City and Ajax build from the back, are patient, play wide, create a pivot, pass in a triangle, and their full-backs play higher up. And, as Cruyff always did as a coach, there's a huge focus on controlled possession. When the opposition attack, they create space. Width is important. Wingers create wide crosses. Crosses create goals and they both have a high-pressing side, so when they lose the ball they press aggressively. It sometimes reads like a back-to-basics manual but it's about passing, possession and controlling the game.

At Ajax, ten Hag hasn't had the same budget as Manchester City so the club focuses on rearing, coaching and bringing through players like Matthijs de Ligt and signing and recruiting players like Frenkie de Jong. He joined from Willem II before starring for Jong Ajax. They moved to Juventus and Barcelona respectively for the same price, 75m Euros. This was how they would generate cash. Like the stars in the 1970s side, they would be coached, given the chance in the first team then sold for huge transfer fees.

In August 2020, Donny van de Beek was sold to Manchester United for £40m. Van de Beek encapsulates every aspect of the

Ajax model. Brought in at the age of 11, he came through the youth academy and was coached through every team and into the first team for a few years before being sold on. Van de Beek is in a long-term relationship with Dennis Bergkamp's daughter, Estelle. She moved to the north-west with him. Bergkamp himself was able to advise him on the transfer. Van de Beek said, 'I have the best possible adviser when it comes to football issues. I know Dennis did not play for the same club as I do now, but I also know that he's a legend in England. He knows everything about all the clubs, the teams, and life as a player in the Premier League.'

It's funny how football is connected.

Chapter 31

'So it was okay to end this way. It had been lovely.'

I FOUND myself connecting with Feyenoord. Up until then, I knew about the club because they were a famous name in Dutch and European football. Their huge stadium hosted European finals and had a tunnel that opened up from the ground. Names like Robin van Persie, Henrik Larsson, Giovanni van Bronckhorst and Wim Jansen played for them. I also knew of the bitter rivalry with Ajax. But when Johan Cruyff joined them in 1983/84 I was amazed.

While poring over this momentous year for the club, I learned so much about Feyenoord, their working-class roots, the ethos of *de Trots van Zuid*, and all things of *the pride of the south*. Watching as many games as possible, reading articles and match reports, I felt part of it. I found myself becoming immersed in that remarkable season. Within a few weeks of starting my research, I had become a fan and was rooting for guys like Peter Houtman, André Hoekstra, Sjaak Troost, Henk Duut, Ben Wijnstekers, Ivan Nielsen, Michel van de Korput, André Stafleu, Andrey Zhelyaskov and Stanley Brard, players I had barely heard off. Then, of course, there was a young Gullit and the legendary Johan Cruyff.

To most fans, Cruyff's year at Feyenoord is a brief anecdote and coda in a wonderful career, when he took the huff and headed to De Kuip with his toys flying from the pram. Cruyff being Cruyff, undoubtedly, there was an element of that in his actions, but he didn't treat it like a lucrative, grandstanding testimonial season. He became fixated with every aspect of the team and it looked like he was the coach, telling team-mates exactly where to stand and play, all while being on the pitch himself. Like he did throughout his career, Cruyff was instructing and pointing. It often looked like he spent most of the game speaking, coaching and directing his team's play, gesturing toward space where the ball should be played.

Watching each game over this season, a familiar shape and structure emerge. Ruud Gullit was on the right wing, playing wide, stretching the play and whipping in crosses to Houtman and the ever-running powerhouse that was Hoekstra.

Cruyff himself still had that acceleration from a standing start, the burst of energy to get past players 15 years younger, which allowed him time to set up for a shot or pass. Cruyff and yes, this is something that may shock you, was too modest to discuss how much influence he had over the side when asked about his time at Feyenoord; he only ever talked about the fun and enjoyment he had that season.

It would have taken Alan Turing and his boffin mates from Bletchley Park decades of confusion trying to solve the enigma that was Johan Cruyff. Sticking with Cruyff was an improbable prospect; he had more twists and turns than a black mamba, speedily slithering around the opposition. Marking him would have been impossible, like trying to untangle a myriad of wires and leads and dozens of intertwined cables behind the TV. The game itself back then was barely recognisable. The players were rough and ready, tackles were hard and unforgiving, and there were few penalties, bookings and red cards. The surfaces too weren't great; riveted, hard, and uneven, yet Cruyff still excelled.

Apart from his trivela pass, another unique skill Cruyff used to great effect in this season was a weird one to explain technically. He would be playing with his left foot on the left side but suddenly shoot with his right foot. When he played with the ball on his right he'd shoot with the left. The best and most famous example of this would be the one the Barca fans christened the 'phantom goal' against Atlético Madrid, when he was on the left and sensationally managed to volley with his right heel.

His balance, poise and swift change of direction were distinctive. His body would be able to dip and swing back to a 45-degree angle as he remained on his feet, keep his eye on the ball and then change direction, and still reach the ball, and score with his left foot. It was back to that determination and willingness to stay on his feet instead of falling on to the concrete of Betondorp.

There's a famous image and piece of video footage of Cruyff playing against Argentina in the 1974 World Cup in their first second-round game. That year saw FIFA introduce a new format. There was no knockout stage but a second-round group stage. Sixteen teams divided into four groups. Eight teams advanced and split into two groups of four, and the group winners faced each other in the final. The second-round goal at first appears unremarkable, by Cruyff's standards, and it could even be described as an average goal. But it encapsulates the skills and attributes which made him, at this point, the best player in the world. It was about balance, agility, speed and elegance.

First, the run was perfectly timed. Not too early, not too late, but on time. It took me a while to understand what Cruyff meant when he continually repeated this mantra, until watching him in this season. His idea of timing and use of space was impeccable and he still had an innate sense of being in the exact right place at the exact right moment. If he hadn't been such a great footballer, he would've made an excellent train driver. This allowed him to get behind the defence, through a central position, then he controlled the ball with the technique to kill it and continue moving with it.

He still had to get around the goalkeeper, Daniel Carnevali, before finishing calmly with a left-footed shot from a tight angle. Cruyff actually scored two goals in this 4-0 win. The second was a perfectly placed right-footed volley, from a tight angle, accurately finding its way through a congested six-yard box. He had an assist too, a wonderful left-foot cross for Johnny Rep to head home, but his first is the one to look back on.

In his season at Feyenoord, he was still doing that distinctive move and change of direction, aged 37. In some games, there were a vast array of shots, passes, lobs, link-ups and goals with his left foot.

Another key element to the successful season was how relaxed and happy the Feyenoord players appeared. When they scored, the side celebrated warmly and wholeheartedly. There were no issues, no bruised egos, and everyone sang from the same song sheet. Even the most ardent Feyenoord diehards, both in the team and on the terraces, had smiles of sheer delight. The camaraderie among players was clear to see, especially towards Cruyff when he scored.

Cruyff was always surprisingly modest to the reaction of his team-mates, remaining businesslike, and there were few similar celebrations like those after his Total Football goal in the 1974 World Cup victory against Brazil. When he did raise his arm to the Feyenoord fans it was more of a thank you to the crowd for their applause. However, even he seemed to recognise each passing game became more of a moment and sensed he might just possibly be going out in style. As the weeks passed, those around him raised their game, playing for him and the team. In February, when Feyenoord defeated Ajax 4-1, Cruyff over-did it a bit with his goal celebration. He left no one in any doubt how delighted he was. Forget being respectful to your former team and the side you've supported your whole life. No, Cruyff walloped in the second goal from a yard out with his left foot and reacted like it was a World Cup winner.

One of the first to join the celebrations, despite growing up in Amsterdam, was Feyenoord fan Ruud Gullit, who in almost every goal runs and jumps on Cruyff, celebrating with that glorious smile. Why Gullit seemed so happy is understandable. Not only were his team playing their best football in years, but he was also learning, watching and being coached by one of the best players to have ever lived.

In this season at Feyenoord, Cruyff proved he was still the best 'team player' among the greats of world football. The journalists across the ages will always discuss and debate the best players. It is to Cruyff's huge disadvantage that he was such a magnificent team player. Alfredo Di Stéfano, Ferenc Puskás, Pelé and Diego Maradona and of late, Lionel Messi and Cristiano Ronaldo are wonderful exciting talents but few would drive their team on and inspire them to raise their game.

When there is a debate about the best players and legends in the game, five or six names always emerge on this list, but Cruyff, not only in terms of his skill and play but by his sheer reach and influence is in my view, the most important. In spreading his philosophy, he was the most visionary footballer, someone who strove to influence and revolutionise the game.

For Cruyff, it wasn't enough to be the best player in the world or the second-best to Pelé of the century. To him, it was about his performance and how he could galvanise and help the team to victory. If one of his wonderful turns or passes created a goal that gained a win, a flourish or pass which happened to excite and entertain, that was merely a by-product of the team's performance. It was always the concept of the team, perhaps that was the Dutch mentality.

Cruyff had a wonderful time playing at Feyenoord. He described it as a party with great players, and everyone playing well. He got on well with his coach, Thijs Libregts, though they would have to as Cruyff was doing his job on the pitch. In April 1984, Feyenoord offered to extend Cruyff's deal. It must have crossed his mind but perhaps he preferred to go out on a high, on his terms. Perhaps the memories of how his previous last game had gone were fresh in his mind.

In this original 'farewell' fixture, a match between Ajax and Bayern Munich in Amsterdam in 1978, he was beaten, battered and knocked senseless. The Germans won 8-0 and infamously decided that testimonial rules were off. When Ajax expected a friendly and high-scoring entertaining draw, Bayern came in full battle mode, as though competing in the European Cup Final, playing like their lives depended on it. German author and football journalist Uli Hesse shed some light on the scoreline, 'Karl-Heinz Rummenigge took to Dutch TV in 2006 to apologise about the 8-0 game. Though Rummenigge did also say Cruyff walked over to Sepp Maier, prior to the match and requested he "play a proper game".' So you could say Cruyff got what he asked for, a proper going over.

For such a huge superstar, with a stellar career, the decision to stop playing was made in the most understated of ways. You would assume a player of this quality would know, during a great epiphany, in a pulsating derby after a wonderful hat-trick with the climax of the *1812 Overture* going off in his head, a cacophony of noise and excitement and in a moment of sheer clarity a voice tells him, 'This is it, time to bow out. It will never be as perfect as this again.' Cruyff's moment was more human. It goes back to the double-header over Easter weekend in the title run-in. On Monday, he was ill with the after-effects of two games in succession. 'After the second match, I felt terrible. I stumbled down the stairs, and couldn't actually get back upstairs. I told Danny, "I can't keep this up. We've got to call it a day. It's over,"' he said. Cruyff reminded us that he was human after all.

Despite the offer of a contract extension, he knew it was time to bow out because his body was telling him. He didn't want a repeat of 1978, 'Five years later the fairytale ended the way it should. At the top. With football and moments that the people at Ajax and Feyenoord still talk about. Prizes were won too. In three years, three national titles and two cups which is as good as it gets. So it was okay to end this way. It had been lovely.'

* * *

When Cruyff's death at the age of 68 was announced in 2016, there was shock, disbelief and a mass outpouring of grief. The football world, as it does, came together quite beautifully to mourn him, particularly at Ajax, Barcelona and Feyenoord. This was despite the football community and the KNVB refusing to employ him as a coach for decades. But that's okay, now's not the time.

As a fan, I was appreciative and thankful that his death was handled in such a comforting and sensitive way. There was a genuine acceptance that Cruyff's death was elevated to a level of significance. This was more than a news story; this felt like something more momentous. Finally, they realised how important this man was. This was like the death of a composer, a great artist or movie director. His passing was regarded and treated as a significant cultural loss, of someone who had contributed greatly to his chosen field. His life and professional career was treated respectfully and re-appraised. Finally, they spoke of him as they would Bowie, Picasso or John Coltrane.

Not only did they recognise, on a human level, the sadness of his passing but also the significance of his impact on his chosen field as a player and coach were highlighted and re-affirmed.

In an interview with Dutch news show *Nieuwsuur*, Henry Kissinger, the politician, diplomat and geopolitical consultant, who served as the US Secretary of State and as a National Security Adviser for presidents Nixon and Ford, was a keen football fan and friend of Cruyff. Now well into his 90s, he had stopped doing any interviews but for Cruyff, he agreed to speak. The Nobel Peace Prize winner spoke fondly about his love of the game and how he received a mysterious letter every Monday in his office and no one ever knew what it was. It turned out to be the football results from that weekend's football from the European leagues. The German office sent them to him in the days long before he could easily check on the internet.

When interviewed and queried about where he was on 3 July 1974, Kissinger was sharp as ever, 'At the semi-final between Holland and Brazil, played in Dortmund. I was in the stadium and I saw Holland win, they played beautifully. It was artistic, it was beautiful to watch.' Kissinger remembered, with clarity, being mesmerised by the way the Dutch played, 'It was the fluidity of the game. It was the way they passed the ball with the expectation that the other player would be at a certain place even though he wasn't there when the ball was passed.'

Kissinger left his best line for an awkward question about Cruyff's diplomacy. Tellingly, skilfully and with all the tact and diplomacy he could muster, he thought through the interviewee's simple but excellent question, 'Would Cruyff make a good diplomat?' Kissinger smiled, 'I think he probably was too dominant to be a good diplomat. As a good diplomat, you have to leave a margin for your adversary. I think Cruyff thought that, with his skill consisting in large part, he had a superior margin over his adversary.'

On the 24 March 2016 edition of BBC show *Newsnight*, presenter Emily Maitlis introduced a news piece about Cruyff's death and the loss as if he was Beethoven or Mozart. He was a cultural icon. She said, 'They talk of him as the man who reinvented football. The Dutch Master, John Cruyff, died today. A player, then a manager who gave a whole new philosophy to football – you might even say gave us the modern inimitable Barcelona as it plays today. Just as importantly he gave us the legacy: the Cruyff Turn.'

The show then moved to a tribute. When we returned, Emily was shown by two youth players how to do a turn, and she was decent too, in heels with a great left foot. Most news items and shows treated his passing with a mix of loss but also a celebration of how he played football.

The man who gave a whole new philosophy to football and reinvented the game did so because he looked at it differently from mere mortals. To him, like the great musician or artist, for the greater good, football had to be witnessed as a thing of beauty. As Mathew Syed explained in his book on success, *The Greatest,* this attitude was pivotal to the way his sides would play, 'When you look at the teams masterminded by Cruyff, both as a player and coach, this truth shines through. Winning was a big thing. And this is why their performances were infused with such imagination and flair. He regarded the pass as not a functional aspect of the game, but as a thing of beauty.'

His son Jordi said, 'I think he's one of those legends whose name is always going to be spoken about, like Pelé, and Maradona, the rest of us are just mortals, we come and we go.'

Sjaak Swaart, who played with Cruyff at Ajax and witnessed him coming through has his theory: 'Johan Cruyff, Maradona, Pelé, Eusébio – they were all fantastic players but Johan was the greatest.'

Frank Rijkaard said, 'It all started with Cruyff and yes, he is the godfather of Dutch football.' Marco van Basten concurred, 'He inspired every youth of Holland, everyone wanted to play like him.'

Joan Laporta said, 'Johan revolutionised the city and the country. He transformed Barcelona and Catalonia because during his time here he turned football into an art form. Johan was innovative and a breath of fresh air.'

* * *

In writing this story, at times I felt it was too far-fetched. Ajax discard Cruyff and, out of sheer rage, he goes to bitter rivals Feyenoord? On the surface it's a great tale but it seems too easy, too contrived and convenient. If you are a fan of Cruyff and understand his nature and mentality, you would understand he would be angry and hurt, more out of professional pride, but wouldn't react in such a way to leave Ajax to be spiteful. Even the money, which on some home gates would have been eye-watering, wouldn't have been enough. Perhaps it was something else. The challenge, maybe? Cruyff was too experienced and too much of a cold-hearted professional.

In the final stages of writing his memoirs and when seriously ill, Cruyff revealed another aspect and strand to the story. He was angry and dismayed, yes, but when he arrived at Feyenoord he was in bits emotionally after the death of his 'second father', his stepfather Henke. This, he explained, affected him more than he would have ever thought, 'In 1983, my stepfather passed away and that loss affected me so badly that my form at Ajax suffered.' So Ajax may have seen his form dip and assumed his mind was elsewhere, or perhaps they thought it was his age, maybe his attitude was wrong or his heart was no longer in it?

Cruyff was adamant that he would not have gone to play football purely out of spite. Pride yes, but not spite: 'I'd like to clear up one misunderstanding. I have never been driven by rancour. Not even in 1983, when I wanted to take out my anger on Ajax via Feyenoord after the club had thrown me out with the garbage.'

In this statement, Cruyff brilliantly denied that it was about retribution while casting it up and reminding everyone of how he felt when Ajax tossed him aside.

Cruyff was skilled at that. There were also other mitigating circumstances in the story, 'The board knew [about the death of Uncle Henke] but the world was told all kinds of implausible stories about me and I was delivered to Feyenoord in a highly damaged state.'

Yet he confirmed that he did use the death of Henke to inspire him, 'After that, I gathered all my resources to end my career in the spirit of my second father. That gave me the incredible strength to win everything there was to win,

Eredivisie, the cup, the Golden Boot. The strength his death unleashed in me surprises me still.'

When reflecting on the inventiveness and ingenuity of the Dutch, the philosopher Rene Descartes said, 'God made the Earth, but the *Dutch* made *Holland*.' If he were ruefully pondering in an Amsterdam cafe these days he might consider, 'God made the Earth, but *Cruyff* made *Holland*.'

Cruyff once famously said, 'I haven't always been understood. As a footballer, as a coach and also for what I did after all that. But okay, Rembrandt and Van Gogh weren't understood either. That's what you learn: people go on bothering you until you're a genius.'

Many contend that Cruyff was a flawed virtuoso. I say he was a fierce genius.

Acknowledgements

Thanks to my wife, Sharron, for her support and editing. This book has been a joy to write, and a labour of love. I would like to thank Paul and Jane at Pitch Publishing for making it such an enjoyable experience. Also Graham Hales, Duncan Olner, Gareth Davis, Dean Rockett and all involved in the making and production of this book.

Finally, thanks to you, and football fans everywhere.

A x

Note on Sources

The author wishes to acknowledge the following sources:

Books
Cruyff, Johan: *My Turn: The Autobiography* (Pan MacMillan, 2016).
Gullit, Ruud: *How to Watch Football* (Viking, 2016).
Winner, David: *Brilliant Orange: The Neurotic Genius of Dutch Football* (Bloomsbury Paperbacks, 2012).
McIlvanney, Hugh: *On Football* (Mainstream Publishing, 1994).
Bergkamp, Dennis: *Stillness and Speed: My Story* (Simon & Schuster, 2014).
Syed, Matthew: *The Greatest* (John Murray, 2017).

Newspapers
The Guardian (especially the work of Donald McRae and Sid Lowe).
Glasgow Herald
The Independent
Daily Mail
De Telegraaf

Movies
Nummer 14 (1972), directed by Maarten de Vos
Johan Cruijff En Un Momento Dado (2004), directed by Ramón Gieling

Documentaries
Football's Greatest: Johan Cruyff, ITV Sport (2015)

Websites
Tifo Football Videos (YouTube)
transfermarkt.com
www.skysports.com